The Rebirth
Of A
Broken Destiny

A Life from Pity to Envy

Lawrence NuBari Maeba

PRESS

Table of Contents

Dedication

*To my beloved wife, NiaBari Blessing Maeba
and my children, Faith Baridakara Maeba
and Favour Lawrence Maeba, who have
all blessed me with love that words cannot
express. I say thank you and I love you back.
To my mother Kpughi Maeba who loved and
cares for eight children including me as a
single mother, you are the best.
This book is also dedicated in memoriam to
my father, Hon. Sampson Basi Maeba
who I loved so much.*

To my elder brother, Mr. Sylvester LeBari Basi Maeba who led me to the path of education, thank you and remain blessed.
To my father in the Lord, Bishop David O. Oyedepo—I will not cease to thank God and bless the day you were born. This work is made possible due to my spiritual connection with you and ministries.

INTRODUCTION

No man was born pitiful, but people do became pitiable creatures when they walk into the wrong environment. The transformation or relocation from the wrong place to the right place is what turns a pitiable child into an enviable king.

Only God can make everything from nothing or make something from anything. Your manifestation is not in your f rst or last name, what you know, or the people you are connected to. It is in the place God has prepared for you.

Every child of God is a bona f de candidate for signs and wonders, and as such, is one to be envied, not pitied. Just as every passenger on an airline f ight is entitled to every meal and service the airline provides to passengers onboard, so it is with the child of God and all good things God provides. It does not matter which "ticket" you have, your age, your color, or where you are seated—you get all promised services. You are automatically qualif ed for every service onboard—as long as you stay on board to be counted.

Wherever there is life, there is hope. Wherever there is faith, there is victory. There is no human situation on earth that has no heavenly solution—if applied as instructed by God.

A man can live his entire life time in error and never know his true value until he encounters a serious life issue. Problems help to expose to you what is missing in your life. If there is one particular thing you are not seeing in your life, problems will expose it. That one thing is keeping you from what God has prepared for you. That one thing is stopping God's blessing from manifesting in your life.

There is no giant bigger than you anywhere. Your giant is the unseen wall standing between you and your destiny. Your ignorance to the truth is what keeps your giant active. John says,

"And ye shall know the truth,
and the truth shall make you free"
(John 8:32).

God is everywhere but He does not bless everyone in the same place. There is a place and a time God has for each and every man on earth and until you are at your place, your success remains a daydream. Many folks are suffering today from different kinds of untold hardship because they cannot locate their rightful place to meet with God. No man is cre-

ated to manifest in every trade, but someone is created for a particular trade—you are at your best doing what you were created to do.

God's divine appointment does not follow people, but waits for the right person at the appointed place for manifestation. It is not a friendly way to live an entire life, doing the wrong thing in the wrong place. Life is too short to wait too long for God to do something. Waiting does not move God. Acting is what God values.

God is not a respecter of color, age, sex, educational background, or earthly connections, but a respecter of faith expressed in the action of doing the right thing.

I made a series of mistakes in my life and wasted several years searching for something I couldn't fnd. I acquired so much in earthly things at a young age, but none of it gave me satisfaction. The more I got, the more I needed.

0

More and more! The more friends I made, the more trouble I had as a result of associations.

One morning, I woke up in my normal cry, recalling the words mama used to tell me every night, when I was still a boy. She used to tell me: "My dear son, life is a journey full of wonders and decisions. The decisions you make at the source determines your destination. No man has made it on planet earth without help from above. Even Jesus Christ, our savior, was in contact always with heaven, which helped him to go through life successfully to the end. He is the only one who can lead you through to the end. Son, accept Jesus as your best friend and the world will be surprised at you how you will walk through life."

I did not know it then, but life is lived in phases, and men in their sizes. I thought it was one's background that made life so comfortable for some, but that is not true at all.

The reason why the prodigal son headed into a far country was to get satisfaction. Instead, he resorted to a life of riotous living that took away all his substance over time and then he suffered lack.

He was an honored, prosperous, and healthy man who was loved by his father. After he left his rightful place to travel to a far country, the Bible says he suffered much hunger, pain, and frustration. He became a slave in a foreign land. Destiny is not built by chance, but by facts. The environment in which you live determines the kind of life you live.

As you read this book and do all you are asked to do, I see you turning back your destiny, in Jesus' name. Amen.

CHAPTER ONE

The Power of Choice

"I call heaven and earth to record this day against you, that I have set before you life and death, blessing and cursing: therefore choose life, that both thou and thy seed may live" *(Deuteronomy 30:19).*

▶ **Choice:** God's love for mankind is amazing. Sadly, man loved the choice to live life according to his own will. God placed before man life and death, blessing and cursing, and still man must choose life so that both he and his seed may live.

Man has the choice of time to die or live, a life of cursing or blessing. We are surrounded by technologies that can end several lives in seconds, things that have no respect for life— when our lives are up to the choice of another man.

It is true that no man, with his f ve senses alone, can measure the size of his problems to be the same with the solutions because that might not be the remedy to his problem.

We live in a world of wonders where fast foods have taken over the pride of a loving wife in the kitchen—the choice to cook and eat food at home or choice to go out for food prepared by others.

What is choice? Choice is simply the right to choose or the chance to choose between two or more things—what you like or don't like. Man has too many choices to make but God offers two primary choices to all man: life or death.

The verse above presents the choice given to man by God. God placed before man the choice of life or death. Man has every right to chose life and live longer or to choose death and die. There is a demand placed on man in the journey of life—a man's choice of how to travel the journey determines how he goes. We all have the demand upon us to say "Yes" or "No" to whatever question we are faced with or come across along life's way.

The marketplace has a wide choice of products from different manufacturers. Business has a wide choice of trades. College offers a wide range of course choices. The government sets laws in place to maintain order—but men must choose to obey or disobey those laws. The instructor holds great knowledge from which he must choose that which is most important for his students to learn. A woman has a wide choice of relationships to keep or to end, and so on. Life offers many choices for man to make that will greatly affect him and his environment.

No one has the choice of what circumstances will occur in their future. In fact, the choice you have to make now could be the last choice you make in life.

As people differ, so do their choices. Everyone has the right to his or her choices in life. God gave man the choice of life or death, blessing or cursing to choose from. God said,

> *"I call heaven and earth to record this day against you, that I have set before you life and death, blessing and cursing: therefore choose life, that both thou and thy seed may live."*
> *(Deuteronomy 30:19)*

This is a very wide choice God has given man to make, for whoever wants to live chooses life, but he that wants to die chooses death.

When you visit a bar, the bartender doesn't just give you any available drink rather he asks for your choice of drink. You might be a regular customer of that particular bar, but he still asks for your choice. You have full rights to whatever drink you choose at that moment. No one can deny you your choice because whatever choice you make is for you and on you. Even when you visit a friend, he or she f rst asks you the kind of drink or food you want after offering you available choices.

Whatever choice you make determines what is given to you, it could be nothing because you have the right to say yes or no to the offer. Responses could be: "Thank you, but I don't need anything at the moment, or "I need just water." Nobody of sound mind would force you to accept what is against your will.

If God does not impose choices on anyone, why should man try to impose choices on his fellow man?

"Go and say unto David, Thus saith the LORD,
I offer thee three things; choose thee one of
them, that I may do it unto thee"
(2 Samuel 24:12).

When you make the choice, God makes the change. You must let go of wrong choices and take hold of right choices that allow God to do His work. Poverty and prosperity are choices to make. One may choose to be poor or choose to prosper.

Many are living as debtors because they chose to purchase on credit an item they could not afford to buy. Though they wisely chose not to steal it, they unwisely chose not to save money to purchase it. They have placed themselves into indebtedness that could last years.

It bothers me so much when I see people envying others for what they have. The choice to own a big car or a small car is a choice. It is a choice to purchase or rent a home—so why the envy? I cannot comprehend this.

"Butter and honey shall he eat, that he may know to refuse the evil, and choose the good"

(Isaiah 7:15).

Everyone has the free will to do good or bad, the choice to be free from or to remain addicted to drugs or sex. When you go shopping, before you decide which product to buy, you f rst compare the qualities, sizes, colors, weights, taste, price and more.

We all have different choices of cloths to wear or food to eat. My choice of food might not be yours. The very car I admire might be the very one you do not like and would never own.

We are very pessimistic in the choices we make in our lives. But what you choose to do today will determine where you end up tomorrow and in the days ahead. Our right choices of the books we read, the music we listen to, and the company we keep; all these can deliver us from destructions.

"He sent his word, and healed them, and delivered them from their destructions"
(Psalms 107:20).

Every day we wake up to see a bright new day. This is a sign that the choice of God continues to be in our favor. Some choices people make put them in the dark. Your choice can free you from debt and your choice can make you a permanent debtor for the rest of your life. Before you make any choice, consider what your priorities are.

"What man is he that feareth the LORD?

him shall he teach in the way

that he shall choose"

(Psalm 25:12).

If you want to drive an expensive car to measure up with others, and all you make is $2,000 a month, along with other expenses—car loan $300, credit cards $200, rent or mortgage $1200, gas and utility bills sum up to $300 a month—all you did is sign up for a loan that will drag you farther and farther behind. How do you expect to progress in life? Your demand for high taste leads to a life of no return. Life becomes so very diff cult to cope with when the income coming in is less than the expenses being paid out.

"Cut your coat according to your size," they say. A beggar may say he has no choice, but when he has even one ability, trade or skill (as everyone does), a beggar has made his choice not to work but to beg. As long as you have something to offer, you have choices.

Always think of where you are coming from and where you want to go before making your choices. This will help guide you in making wise choice. No man was born a fool. His bad choices are what qualify him to be a fool. Our personal character is formed by the choices we make.

▸ **Decision:** Our decision-making process and habits decide the kind of choices we make in our daily lives. We all make different kinds of choices depending on the decisions we make. Many are spending their lives in prison as a result of wrong decisions they made, often in ignorance. It takes only a second to make and act on a decision, but the end result depends on the source by which that decision was made. Our individual decisions dictate for us the choices to make. The wise man weighs what the end of any decision will bring to himself and others.

"Hope deferred maketh the heart sick:
but when the desire cometh, it is a tree of life"
(Proverbs 13:12).

Ungodly decisions have never given anyone a happy end. No wonder you hear people that make ungodly decisions say: "I decided to quit the marriage relationship" or, "I decided to stop serving God" or, "I decided to kill or steal" because "there was no other option for me."

One secret the devil uses to make us victims of his devices is his involvement in our decision making. He knows that a split second decision can destroy decades of achievement. We should be very careful of who we allow to come f rst in our decision making. It can take only a second to fall, then years to get back up.

The king said,

"The fear of the LORD is the beginning

of knowledge: but fools despise

wisdom and instruction"

(Proverbs 1:7).

This connotes the idea on which your action is based and the environment in which you are making the decision and upon whose instructions you will stand. Be wise in your decision making.

▶ ***The Narrow Way:*** "Jesus, I come to you today out of my bondage, my sorrow, my distress and darkness. I come to you out of my shameful addiction, out of my loss and repeated failures, and out of my restlessness and arrogant pride. Jesus, I come into your Kingdom where gladness and glory prevail."

"Come unto me, all ye that labour and are heavy laden, and I will give you rest"
(Matthews 11:28).

"I come into thy balm, thy health, love, peace, calmness, wealth and joy. With open hands and heart I come to you, to recover all that has been mysteriously taken from me by a mighty storm. There is no one like you Lord Jesus, I've come to anchor with you and I pray no wind will pull me out of you. I have been rejected by men in the world but you accepted and restored me.

I have no place to lay my head on earth. The enemy's mouth is open to swallow me, but at thy word I know that I am saved."

The narrow way of life is always under construction. It never gets smoother for any man. When it seems too hard to walk, it takes courage and patience to walk on.

The narrow way is very hard to f nd. It is not popular, way far from the main streets—it has no physical direction. The narrow way has no place for high life; it is the way that humbles everyone that passes through. Those on the narrow way don't normally invite visitors because it is not a place for fun or a place to be lightly reckoned with. It is a long and lengthy path to follow but it leads to life eternal. It is rough at the beginning but the end thereof is smoother.

Everyone wants the end glory of the narrow way, but no one wants to be part of walking it through to the end.

"Strive to enter in at the strait gate: for many, I say unto you, will seek to enter in, and shall not be able"

(Luke 13:24).

Many have chosen to walk the narrow path, but couldn't make it to the end. Very few make it to the end. It takes faith, patience, consistent focus, endurance, and conf dence to walk on the narrow way. The narrow way is not a place for a celebration party. The narrow way is a time in the night season when you do not see any joy coming (at least not soon).

▶ *Attitude:* The choice of attitude plays an essential role in the life of a man. What is an attitude? Attitude is the way one behaves or reacts towards another or toward a given situation. One must be careful in his choice of attitude in respect to the law of harvest. The Bible says "do unto others what you will welcome from others"

> "Therefore all things whatsoever ye would that
> men should do to you, do ye even so to them:
> for this is the law and the prophets"
> (Matthew 7:12).

What you give to others is the same you shall be given by others. What you wish others will become today determines what you will become tomorrow.

The attitude of a man determines his relationship with others. Do good to others and good shall be paid back to you in return (often from where you do not expect). Your attitude must agree with the thoughts and will of others to be in good relationship with them. You are known by your attitude towards others on the job, in the classroom, and in the church. No matter how highly anointed you may be, your attitude has a vital role to play in keeping you either on the throne of grace's blessing or f at down in the grass from grace's reproof.

The attitude of a man affects the words he speaks. The mouth, as we all know, is very pretty in shape, located at a very unique position on the body. The mouth can be used 24/7 without running out of words, so it is very dangerous if not properly used. Good attitudes build trust for a man. When a man possesses a good attitude, he creates the kind of reputation that gives him an internal peace in every area of his life which extends to those around him. Good attitudes give a clear direction to the place of honor and achievement, with no regret or failure. It also opens him up in terms of making intelligent choices and decisions.

You can change your attitude but cannot change your face or color. Always do the best you can to f ow in peace and harmony with people you encounter in your life.

" *If it be possible, as much as lieth in you,*
live peaceably with all men"
(Romans 12:18).

Talking about attitude, this story taught me a lesson I will live to remember:

A female nurse was f red by her boss because she was seen by him as the only one qualif ed in her off ce to replace her boss. But she treated her poorly and f red her. A month later, she was employed in another hospital as director. Three months later, her former boss that f red her originally came to her off ce to interview for a job—only to see the woman she had f red was now a director in that department! She ran away!

Wrong attitudes echo out in your words to people. You cannot possess a bad attitude and be an encourager to others, so try to pose a loving attitude as not to be self deceiver. Let people see you also do what you tell them to do or live the very kind of life you want them live.

"But be ye doers of the word, and not hearers

only, deceiving your own selves"

(James 1:22).

When you have rewarding thoughts for life, you become what your words say. When your words for life are positive, you become a role model for others. When you respond wisely to situations, you are set to become a reformer who not only rebuilds the desolate places, but one who inspires the brokenhearted and restores hope to the hopeless people.

When your behavior toward others is welcoming, you become a friend to them. When your character pleases others, you become a problem solver because everyone around you will love to share their personal issues with you since they have come to know you as a people person—someone who cares.

The thoughts you allow to keep f ashing through your mind will settle in your mind and form what comes out of your mouth or what become your actions. The fruits of your mouth birth your actions. Repetition of an act forms the basis for your attitudes. All of this works together to form your character which, if poorly handled, could lead you to your pitiable end. Be watchful over your thoughts.

You have all it takes to acquire all you need or want. You can control your attitude, if after every meeting you have with people, you try to ask yourself how fair or rude you were in that meeting. This will reveal to you the impression you left of yourself to others.

It is true that attitude can make a man, but attitude can also break the same man. Attitude is a very crucial part of our everyday lives that should be checked and balanced at all times.

No matter how highly anointed or placed a man may be, without good relationships with people around him, he isn't valued worth a dime in society. Once you sense your attitude stinking, take time out to f x it immediately.

"Keep thy heart with all diligence; for out of it
are the issues of life.

Put away from thee a froward mouth, and
perverse lips put far from thee."
(Proverbs 4:23-24).

Jesus Christ, with all the anointing that was upon Him and His good attitude with the people was able to pull crowds everywhere he went. His attitude boosted Him to be a hero through His miraculous acts. Attitude is more important than physical appearance and skills. Attitude can build or destroy a family, church, business, or organization. A man's life story is graded about 15% on what he encounters and 85% on how he reacts to it. It is true that a man may be a professor in public relations and still not have good relationships; even within his own household.

Good attitude is what singles out a man for the favor of God and man. A man of good attitude is a man of intellect, a man of high value, a good thinker, a man of peace. Good attitudes keep one from trouble and bad relationships. Take a moment to ref ect on your attitude. It might not be as perfect as you think.

► ***The Little At Hand*:** In life, there is a time of plenty and a time of little, but better is the little you have at hand with the fear of God than giant wealth today and getting into trouble deeply tomorrow.

The journey of life is a journey that is best travelled with this in mind as a guiding thought: "Value what is present before you. Forget the past and what is to come."

What you can see is what you can get. When you are thankful with the little at hand, you show the giver that what is past and yet to come is up to Him. Value and make good use of whatever you have at hand. Take advantage of the slightest chance you have to be the best because the journey ahead might not be offered to you a second time. Hold onto whatever you have at hand and thank the giver. Remember, there are millions waiting to get even that little that you have. Keep your eyes away from things you don't have. What you don't have is not for you. Life is not all about struggles. If struggle were the mother of greatness or achievement, many more people would have hit the f nish line in wealth.

The success of the journey ahead lies in knowing the right thing to do and doing it at the right time and at the right place. That is all you need for a victorious journey.

Many are busy praying for more and more, forgetting that the journey ahead demands daily breád.

The road ahead demands every man to be careful not to play with God's commandments. When a man disobeys God's order, he vexes His righteous soul and turns the loving and mer-
ciful Creator a killer. The story of Pharaoh and the Israelis tells us how the same Red Sea that delivered the Israelites turns a killer to Pharaoh and his soldiers, due to their disobedience to

God. This experience tells us how God blessed some and cursed others in the same city.

The road ahead is a road that blesses those who obey the commandments of God. God promises to hear and deliver anyone in trouble that calls upon Him. But many are swimming in the pool of trouble every day, and even when they call upon God, they see no sign to show them God hears them. Some even get the impression that things got worse after they called upon God.

God is not a liar, but many in trouble still accuse Him of being a liar when things don't go right as they desire. They forget that their failure to do right is often the reason for their failure to receive God's blessing.

CHAPTER TWO

The Unveiling Secret in One Day

"For a day in thy courts is better than a thousand. I had rather be a doorkeeper in the house of my God, than to dwell in the tents of wickedness"

(Psalm 84:10).

► **One Day:** There are many days in one's life, but there is a certain day that shines above the rest days. Every day is not the same that is why each day has a unique name. Many are struggling to get through their days when they should be asking God for a day that is better than a thousand.

What makes your day better or worse is your foundation. A single day in a man's life can put all the policemen in a nation on the streets, bring sadness, or start a war. While a single day in a man's life can bring joy to not only his nation, but to the entire world.

Everyone has the opportunity to make a day shine above the others in life. As others make their days worse, you can make your day a blessing not just to yourself, but to an entire generation. You are born for a particular day in life, you might live for one hundred years, but you have only one day to fulfll your mission on earth.

It came to a stage in my life when everything naturally turned against me and I began questioning many issues in life. One early morning of a bright new day, I woke up singing a new song of one day. I was continually meditating in my heart on these two words, "one day." As that continued, I started confessing it with my mouth.

This became a serious issue in my life and with my family. I was always saying it, so my daughter Faith joined me in saying it. When my wife asked me, "What is the meaning of this 'one day' and why are you and Faith always saying it?" I was unable to give her a meaningful answer, save this, that there are days, and then there comes a day that is labeled "one day." There is one day in the life of every man to fulfll his mission on earth.

"One day" became the talk of the day in our home. It dominated all other sayings. I knew there must be something to this "one day" that I needed to know more about, so I went on a three day search on "one day." I left my family to settle the pressing issue about one day, taking a three day journey to the mountain top. For two days, I was in the Bible and on my knees praying for revelation on "one day."

On the third day there, I was given a book containing an endless paragraph. As I opened it page by page, God was revealing to me the hidden blessings in "one day": the uncovered stories in one day, the mighty power in one day, the unseen testimonies and more. I was seeing things many men wished to know, but had no clue where to press in to f nd answers, so it had remained only a daydream for them.

I strongly believe God that this revelation coming to you now will answer many long-awaited question you have about your relation-ships, career, business, profession, or in your family and personal life.

Life is full of challenges. Only those people with links to the Creator are qualif ed for winning the challenges in health, wealth, family relationships, daily endeavors and so on.

A winner does not emerge at the beginning of a contest, the winner is only known at the end of every game. It is the same in life. Great men are not born they are made through tireless work to make it happen. One day doesn't just come to be. One day occurs once in the entire life of a man; hast thou not heard?

But, beloved, be not ignorant of this one thing, that one day is with the Lord as a thousand years, and a thousand years as one day.

The Lord is not slack concerning his promise, as some men count slackness; but is longsuffering to us-ward, not willing that any should perish, but that all should come to repentance.

But the day of the Lord will come as a thief in the night; in the which the heavens shall pass away with a great noise, and the elements shall melt with fervent heat, the earth also and the works that are therein shall be burned up"
(2 Peter 3:8-10).

One day is pregnant and until you get into one day, you have no clue what is contained in it. God is no respecter of persons. There is a day in the life of every man for the manifestation of the Lord, the verse above said it will come "as a thief in the night" meaning that no man had any formal announcement of its coming. No man needed a thousand years to be what God has for him; it is for a day of divine visitation and that settles it.

The God we serve is a God of creative confession. He speaks things to be the way He wants them be. It wouldn't take God more than one day to speak all He wants you to be, and everything he said would come into manifestation. That is why, when God visits a man, it takes less than a day for him to start manifesting. After Jesus speaks into the life of Bartimaeus, the blind man, and people saw him, now with sight regained, and gave praises unto God. Some said he looks like the former blind man but were not sure if he was the same man.

"The neighbors therefore, and they which before had seen him that he was blind, said, Is not this he that sat and begged?

Some said, This is he: others said, He is like him: but he said, I am he"
(John 9:8-9).

The man was born blind, lived in total blindness for many years; until that one day. When his day came, it took him less than a minute to receive his sight, miraculously.

Those who knew this man couldn't believe their eyes! Some said he looked like the blind man, but must not be. But then the man identified himself as the man who had been blind— verifying that he could now see. Praise the Lord!

The Lord showed me in that same book, that complaining and crying was just a waste of time and energy. They were not going to change my situation or make it better. He said I should only pray for the grace to see my day come as He has promised me. He told me to focus on Him and to keep my eyes and mind from the things I do not have. Whatever I don't have is simply not for me.

I pray you will change your prayer focus now to asking God for the grace to live to see your one day come to pass.

"To everything there is a season,

and a time to every purpose under the heaven"

(Ecclesiastes 3:1).

God predetermines the events of life from the beginning of the world but here we are, with celebrated self-conf dence wanting to jump-start the processes of life. Jesus Christ, the only beloved son of God, born in the world with revelations of his greatness to humanity and to the world—yet even he waited patiently for his time to fully come, before putting into action all the revelations He had been given.

There is time and season for every event of life. Joseph was thrown in a pit and left to die by his brothers, endured slavery, became the overseer of Pharaoh's household, and then was thrown into prison before ascending to his throne of greatness. Many of us want to be like Joseph, the prime minister of Egypt, but we do not want to go through what he went through to get there. Jesus went through it stage by stage before he was qualif ed to be called great and at the end he said "It is f nished."

The problems and the "heat" we experience in society today are all man-made. We want to see and hear the glory, but not the story. All we want now is testimonies and not stories. Once he was blind but now he can see. No one cares to know why and how long he has been blind. That is part of the story. We only learn from the story. There is a day labeled "one day" for you—it is not over yet.

"Boast not thyself of tomorrow; for thou
knowest not what a day may bring forth"
(Proverbs 27:1)

The person dancing does not see his or her own back. It is the spectators that see the dancer's back. Let another man's lips praise you or criticize you. Do not do so from your own mouth.

Thank God for what you have today and struggle not for what you will eat tomorrow. No soldier predicts how the battle ahead will end. Jesus told His disciples to pray for the day's daily bread, not tomorrow's bread. Your level of preparation determines the content of your day. Many prepared for their one day to come, but very few make it to their days.

I met a man in a prayer meeting who said, "I am not supposed to be in this prayer meeting because my daughter just graduated from high school today. The tradition of all our family members is to be in the party house tonight."

I said to him: "You should be glad to see a day like this in your life because many worked and planned for a day like yours, but never lived to witness one. This is your chance to thank God for seeing yours come to be. Many events that occurred in people's lives teach us what life is really all about. Some people died just a few minutes into their one day. Others died a day before or after their one day. Some even died on their one day. I am talking about a day of manifestation, a day you live to reference forever after in your life."

I f nished addressing the young man and from that moment his feelings changed for better—just as your feelings are changing now, after dwelling on this book of life. Thank God for where you are and struggle not for where you are yet to be. There is a big gap between "be" and "to be," and between here and there, and between now and then. Boast of what you have at hand, not what you are yet to get.

Whatever is present before you is greater than what is behind or ahead of you. The reason why the front windshield of an automobile is wilder than the rear is for the driver to set his focus on the journey ahead—not the one behind.

"I must work the works of him that sent me,

while it is day: the night cometh,

when no man can work."

(John 9:4)

Every reaction starts with an action. There is no reward without an award. Start now on your journey to fulfll the vision and dreams the Lord has given to you while life exists, because a time is coming when the opportunity will not be there for you to grab. Take advantage of every opportunity that comes your way and ask heaven frst what it is.

There is healing in one day. There is break-through in one day. There is revelation in one day. There is restoration in one day. Revival is awaiting your arrival in your one day.

Thus saith the LORD to his anointed, to Cyrus,

whose right hand I have holden, to subdue

nations before him; and I will loose the loins of

kings, to open before him the two leaved gates;

and the gates shall not be shut;

I will go before thee, and make the crooked

places straight: I will break in pieces the gates

of brass, and cut in sunder the bars of iron:

And I will give thee the treasures of darkness,

and hidden riches of secret places, that thou

mayest know that I, the LORD, which call thee

by thy name, am the God of Israel.

(Isaiah 45:1-3)

And there is promotion in one day.

"For promotion cometh neither from the east,

nor from the west, nor from the south"

But God is the judge: he putteth down one,

and setteth up another

(Psalm 75:6-7).

It will take just one day for you to be announced for the promotion God has assigned to you. He said to me, "There are hidden covenants of blessings in 'one day' and only those who f nd them will have them."

It only takes the grace of God upon a man to have a day called one day in his life. May you not miss your one day, because it comes once in a lifetime. Many are struggling day by day to see their one day come true in their lives, but very few live to see one day in their lifetime.

One day brings blessings to the righteous and delivers curses to the wicked.

► *Dream:* Focus is one of the many weapons which make a dreamer victorious. Check this; when God created man, He matched him with his environment and made available whatever man would need to survive and live well. God created man in His image, meaning that man is God in "looks" and capable to doing whatever God can do, if he believes in himself. It takes belief to achieve a dream and focus is the mother of belief.

Dreams are what provoke a life of wonders. Man is in the shape and size God wants him to be. But man, instead of focusing on what he has, went about living in the past and keeping in memory what he didn't have. No mountain is too high and no valley is too low. Dwelling on things you don't have cannot help you achieve your dream. No matter where you are or what you don't have, you are better off than billions of people around the world.

Quit listening to what people are saying about you. Do everything possible to be yourself and to be what God has made you to be. Don't try to be what people say you should be. No matter what or where you are, some people will feel the need to talk about you. Grow past your impossibilities and confdently grow into your dream. Stir up your God- given talents to do the extraordinary.

You can only do what is natural, but God can help you do the supernatural. You are not alone. The fngers and eye of God are all over you. He promises to be with you always, even unto the end of the world. Do not give up on your dream, Stay away from dream killers. Have no contract or contact with them. God does care about you.

He has you in mind to prosper you and to give you a life free of sickness and disease.

Whatever you cannot do for yourself, start today putting your mind and hands to doing something—time is not on your side.

"Whatsoever thy hand findeth to do,

do it with thy might; for there is no work, nor

device, nor knowledge, nor wisdom, in the

grave, whither thou goest."

(Ecclesiastes 9:10)

What is this dream? Among my many def ni-tions, a dream is "the picture of the glorious will of God for man." The result of whatever dream you have depends on your understanding and the interpretation. I am not talking about the kind of dream where you fall asleep and see yourself living in the White House, nor driving a big car, and it ends once you wake up. It is.

the divine understanding of your dream which gives you the audacity to take control over every situation in which you f nd yourself.

> *And the LORD answered me, and said, Write*
> *the vision, and make it plain upon the tables,*
> *that he may run that readeth it."*
> *(Habakkuk 2:2)*

Have a dream and pass the test. There is no dream without a test and a set time for its manifestation. We are in the dreamer's world. Only dreamers are qualif ed to live in this present generation; because only they have the solutions the world is looking for. Dreamers don't hide from history; they birth history, no matter the age. They are part of every change because they create change.

I do not know to which area life is driving you. You might be thinking it is over for you, that success has eluded you; even that God has given up on you. The good news is that your case or situation is not as bad as that of Job or Joseph when they were pressing through on their way to their throne.

God is not a respecter of time or personality. Lazarus was dead and buried for four days, but when the Lord visited his grave, his story changed.

Your trial or tribulation is your prerequisite for your promotion. There is no promotion without a test and every test begins with a dream. Only dreamers are qualif ed to be tested. Dreamers don't go looking for trouble, but trouble looks for them. Because they are space setters, they rejoice in the midst of trials because they see the trial period as a training period.

Dreamers don't see problems in any way; they interpret problems and use the answers to f ght on. Dreamers are reformers who build the desolate places; those who f ght to defend the truth with the wisdom gotten from above that is above all earthly forces.

The more dreams you have, the more your trials will increase. The dream is what gives color to a man in battle. The dream is what transforms a pitiful man into a man who is envied among men—even making them inter-national f gures.

God has not programmed any man or woman for failure. The reason why we weep in the midst of trials is because we lack a picture of God's plan for our lives.

> *"For I know the thoughts that I think toward*
> *you, saith the LORD, thoughts of peace, and*
> *not of evil, to give you an expected end."*
> *(Jeremiah 29:11)*

There is an expected end for every living being that is designed by God. Trials can only delay it, but cannot deny it.

Your dream of one day is what qualif es you for triumph (envy) in the midst of the storm. You don't go looking for trouble, but because you have a dream, trouble will come knocking on your door. Whether you open your door or not, trouble will visit you without announcement. You must go through it in order to qualify for your throne.

Trials come in different forms. Job suffered a total loss—his family, his wealth and his health. Father Abraham and his wife Sarah were faced with barrenness, unable to bear a child. When their child was born, Abraham was asked by God to sacrif ce the very same, long-awaited son, Isaac. Jesus Christ went through the cross and tomb. Moses was a rejected man. David lost his entire family and all his property. In all cases the end of their trial was all in their favor.

The world is getting crazier every day. Wickedness is on the rise. Everyone is praying for the manifestation of dreamers that will birth solutions to the troubles of society. Joseph was one of the solution providers in his day. Without Joseph, there would be no Egypt today, as the nation would not have survived that great famine.

"Is anything too hard for the LORD? At the time appointed I will return unto thee, according to the time of life, and Sarah shall have a son."

(Genesis 18:14)

Nothing whatsoever is too hard for the Lord. When the appointed time (one day) comes, your life will forever be a blessing not to you alone, but to everyone around you. Catch a dream and live life with it because a man's dream is the foundation of his future. Dreamers don't give up in any situation, no matter how strong or threatening it seems. Dreamers are situation changers; they are name changers.

"And he said, Let me go, for the day breaketh.

And he said, I will not let thee go,

except thou bless me.

And he said unto him, what is thy name?

And he said, Jacob.

And he said, Thy name shall be called no more

Jacob, but Israel: for as a prince hast thou

power with God and with men,

and hast prevailed."

(Genesis 32:26-28)

Every change of situation brought about change of name because old wine is not permitted to be stored in a new wineskin. One great man in blessed memory, Dr. Martin Luther King, Jr. said "I have a dream." That dream changed a whole nation and it is still speaking to this day (and will speak forever).

A dreamer can die, but his dream lives forever. "Nigerian Government can kill the messenger but cannot kill the message," said Late Ken-Saro Wiwa – in his address to the Ogonis in Bori. Dreamers are mountain movers. They don't line up in the hospital to see doctors. Instead, they go to the hospitals to provide solutions for the sick. They don't vie for political off ce, but they tell the government what to do and how things should be. The dreamers of our days are not only those who can read and write, but thinkers; those who use their minds properly and powerfully.

▶ ***Focusing on One Day:*** Dreamers focus on what is ahead, not on what is present. Only those who see ahead get ahead. There is something bigger ahead. Those who don't see ahead, die ahead. No matter what kind of situation you are facing now, it is just temporal. Look ahead for your one day because it must surely come. Though it may tarry, wait for it and be expectant.

You will be the head and not the tail, you must get ahead to be the head. The difference between the head and the tail is that the head is ahead while the tail is behind. Dreamers are heroes. They are award winners. They are always pregnant with solutions that make history and build mansions on solid rock.

Again, the devil taketh him up into an

exceeding high mountain, and sheweth him all

the kingdoms of the world, and

the glory of them;

And saith unto him, All these things will I give

thee, if thou wilt fall down and worship me.

Then saith Jesus unto him, Get thee hence,

Satan: for it is written, Thou shalt worship the

Lord thy God, and him only shalt thou serve.

Then the devil leaveth him, and, behold,

angels came and ministered unto him.

(Matthew 4:8-11)

You cannot see ahead and not be ahead. In his trial, Jesus saw what awaited him ahead of what the devil was offering Him. He was ahead, both spiritually and physically. Jesus was a professional dreamer. He's gone to heaven, but his dream is still ruling the earth until now and will rule forever. The Christian race could have been dead by now if not for the dreamer's victory. Jesus became the overall hero for not accepting the devil's offer—that was not real. Dreamers cannot be bribed to kill their dreams.

No wonder Jesus turned down the devil's earthly offer. Jesus saw beyond the kingdoms of the world and the glory of them and now he's known and addressed as the King of Kings and the Lord of Lords. What a great dreamer? He changed and restored the lost glory of humanity and redeemed man from the pit of sorrow to the throne of authority, far above every principality and power.

Joseph the dreamer faces the bitter part of life, but his dream was always alive and focused upon God. From slave to farmer to house keeper, he ended up spending thirteen years in prison for saying "No" to an offer of sex from Potiphar's wife (and her false claim of sexual attack). The interesting part was that, in all his trials, the favor of God was always upon Joseph, anywhere he was. Even in the prison, he soon came to be the leader of all the prisoners. Dreamers don't cry when trials come. Instead, they face them and turn them to their advantage.

Joseph spent thirteen good years in prison for an offense he didn't commit. The devil planned to end his dream. But it was against the law of the dream to die as a result of the attack. He lost all these years in prison with no clue if or when his freedom would come. I don't know in which area of your life you feel have been denied your dream, but the amazing word is that God is on your side.

▸ **The Manifestation of One Day:** When your day comes, God will use any person or event to bring about your freedom.

"And it came to pass in the morning that his spirit was troubled; and he sent and called for all the magicians of Egypt, and all the wise men thereof: and Pharaoh told them his dream; but there was none that could interpret them unto Pharaoh."

(Genesis 41:8)

Pharaoh had a natural dream and for two full years, the Bible says there was no one to interpret the dream for Pharaoh. Then one day, he became angry that no one was able to tell him what his dream meant. He gathered all the magicians and wise men in Egypt at the time, but none could provide the answer Pharaoh was seeking.

This is when the favor of God upon Joseph "announced" him in the midst of the greatest men in Egypt. Joseph had been in prison for thirteen years, but in all that time, believed his help would come from God one day. He had no idea which direction the help was coming, from man or God, but he maintained his focus on God as his judge who would judge him and set Him free one day. He helped a lot of other prisoners and they forgot about him, but he never fell into self-pity. He always did unto others what he wanted them do unto him.

It came to pass one day that Joseph was sent for by the king. The f rst thing Joseph did was to acknowledge the foundation upon which he stood and the one who was the source for his ability to interpret dreams.

Pharaoh told him all his dreams, not minding that he was speaking to a prisoner. He saw Joseph as a problem solver and the long awaited answer who had been delivered into his hands. The answer was good in the eyes of Pharaoh and all his servants.

After he f nished speaking to Pharaoh, perhaps Joseph was expecting to be returned
to his prison cell, but the Spirit of God was
moving, arranging how Joseph would head up
the vision which was about to manifest. By the
custom of the land of Egypt (and in every other
nation on earth at the time), only a true citizen
of a nation is qualify to be appointed for any
leadership position of that country. Joseph was
not even supposed to be considered to be a
leader.

I am so pleased to announce to you now
that all you need is the favor of God and not the
human connection people are always dying to
get (but that rarely comes).

Joseph did not know that he was only a few
hours away from being the next prime minister
of Egypt. As the arrangement process continued, Joseph had no conviction in his mind
that he would be a leader until the minute he

was promoted to leadership, second in command only to Pharaoh over the land of Egypt (the land he had come to as a slave).

Joseph was appointed to be the ruler over the land of Egypt. Your dream will announce you when your day comes. The same place you are rejected is the same place God will use you to be the selected. The same people that said you would not amount to anything in life are the same people God will bring your way for your help. This shows them that no word a man speaks will come to pass when the Lord has not spoken.

"And Joseph was the governor over the land, and he it was that sold to all the people of the land: and Joseph's brethren came, and bowed down themselves before him with their faces to the earth."
(Genesis 42:6)

This is where the manifestation of Joseph's dream came to pass. All, including his family, bowed down before him. They all lived to see come to pass the very dream that caused others to envy Joseph. You must get there...in Jesus' name.

CHAPTER THREE

Living in Divine Plan

▶ **God's Plan:** the process and battle for life start from the very moment a child is born. The great achievement in the life of each person is the accomplishment of a dream. Dreams are growing by the day, but just a few people are accomplishing them, and very few dreamers live to see their dreams come true or come alive. Anyone that attempts to drive a car with a bad steering column is only trying to commit suicide and to endanger other people's lives. Knowing the plan of God for your life is what keeps one on track to a great destiny. A life outside the plan of God is the same as a great mansion without a foundation. A journey without divine plan is a life without focus and a life without a future.

"Ye are the salt of the earth: but if the salt have lost his savour, wherewith shall it be salted? it is thenceforth good for nothing, but to be cast out, and to be trodden under foot of men."
(Matthew 5:13)

A man on this journey of life without a written plan of God for his life is like a letter in the hand of a mailman with no address. The letter is of no use. When you plan to live life without divine plan, others will give you a plan. Life cannot exist without a plan.

Salt is known for one particular function— to bring out the f avor in the food we eat. You can spend over a thousand dollars on a pot of food, but fail to add that quarter cent's worth of salt and that food will embarrass you before your guests. The food will be good for nothing because the taste will drive away your guests.

If I told you I have some salt, but no taste; what would be your reply? "Trash it!" When salt loses its taste it is also good for nothing. In fact, it is even dangerous for the food because it causes rot. Without the taste, nobody would need salt for anything.

There are so many people today who are lost in life or who live as "good for nothing" because they have no reason for being alive. They are not useful for anything good. The more you try to redirect such people, the less attention you get in return.

▶ *The Prophet:* There are many ways of killing a man physically. Using negative words on someone is another way of killing a man because negative words reduce the value of the person. People can say all sorts of negative words about you and you can still live the life God has for you if you focus on what God said about you and not on what people are saying about you. You only become what they say when you listen and settle on what they say as being true of you.

Prophets are not the mightiest physically, but they are anointed. You have the address of where you are going, but you still need a GPS to direct you point by point to your destination. In the same way, you need someone to interpret the Word of God for you.

Beware of those who come to you to gossip or to recount the bad words others said about you. In the same way, that person goes to gossip about you to others—telling them what you said about them. No matter what they say about you or do to you, be it physically, spiritu-ally, or emotionally, remember God still has a good plan to make you more than a conqueror.

"Shew me thy ways, O LORD;

teach me thy paths.

Lead me in thy truth, and teach me: for thou art

the God of my salvation; on thee do

I wait all the day."

(Psalm 25:4-5)

Give yourself to prayer. Pray for the leading of the Lord for your life. Those who live long are those who know the paths of the Lord for their lives. In prayer, ask God to show you His ways and teach you His paths. Keep your focus on God and wait on Him all day. In this way, you will keep your mind and attention off what people are saying and keep it focused on the plan of God for your life.

Only what you believe has control over you. That is why you must believe what God said about you to be where He has assigned you to be.

"He that receiveth a prophet in the name of a prophet shall receive a prophet's reward; and he that receiveth a righteous man in the name of a righteous man shall receive a righteous man's reward."

(Matthew 10:41)

Prophets are men sent by God to interpret His plans for His children. Prophets decode the coded words of God so we can truly understand what God has for us. The prophets are road maps for us to our divine destinies. They direct and lead us to our promised land. To really connect with a prophet, you must know and receive him as a man sent by God to reveal to you the plans of God for your life.

Everyone needs a prophet or spiritual father (as some call them). Each person is assigned to a particular prophet. My prophet might not be yours. Your prophet determines your habits and the paths you follow in life. You can grow past your college professor, but you cannot grow past your spiritual teacher.

To have a prophet's reward, you must recognize, believe, honor and obey your prophet. The difference between you and your destiny is your prophet. He has the direction you need to reach your destination, and only he can get you there. You might not like his ways, but there is one reason for following him.

▶ **Man's Proposal:** Surviving life in a world of wonders where a man can no longer depend on his own plan anymore is just a daydream for many. God's plan is the one to depend upon. You never can tell which way God has for you until you call upon Him.

> *"Call unto me, and I will answer thee, and show thee Great and mighty things, which thou knowest not."*
>
> *(Jeremiah 33:3)*

This is God confrming his covenant with man. Man should call unto Him and He will answer and show him great and mighty things which he knows not. There are many hidden things man "knows not." Men depend on their own plans day after day (which hardly manifests), not knowing the ways of God are not the ways of man. You cannot survive life in this world of wonders without walking in the plan of God for your life. The only life of wonders is the life which walks in the manifestation of God's will.

The very f rst step in knowing the hidden things of God is to call unto God until He answers. When He answers, he will show you things for your tomorrow you did not know before. The will of God is best for everyone because it is for good and not for evil. It might look uncomfortable for you at the beginning, but stay put and bear whatever you see, for the end must surely be in your favor.

For six years now I still cannot recall the moment I took money from my wallet to pay for my Bible school application forms, though many brothers and sisters in the church tried to sell me the forms, I said no repeatedly to their offers.

There had been several announcements in the church that interested candidates could purchase the forms, but I never saw Bible school as a place for me. I thought it was just for bishops and pastors, not me. I never planned to be one of the interested candidates for Bible school.

Then one night, I found the Bible school application form on my reading desk at home! An audible voice came from the form, saying "f ll me and return me to the church off ce." I walked away from it but could not sleep that night. I spent all night thinking how the form could have gotten to my house.

Throughout the following week, the voice followed me everywhere I went. Finally, I f lled out the form and submitted it—the last application form they accepted before the beginning of classes. I got to class the very f rst day and we were asked to introduce ourselves and give the reason why we chose to attend Bible school.

The f rst student happened to be an attorney, the second a very successful CEO of a well-known organization, and the third student was a medical doctor—it went on and on. Finally, it was my turn and all the things I wanted to say— how I never knew why I was there—became words of wonders. As the courses progressed, I began to know that it was a divine plan for me to be there. It must have been the will of God for me to go through the process of knowing His Word, after surviving several storms of life.

My life before then was at a crossroad. There was no hope of seeing the next day for me. Every day, I woke up to try and see a kind of wonder for me, but God who knows better than man, was at work in my life. Blessed be God. The whole process is now testimonies for others to learn from. It wasn't my plan to go through Bible school in life because I was walking in my plan. But God, being who He is, saved my life from continuing its misguided path. I proposed an easy pathway for my life, but God disposed of my plan and gave me His.

The very f rst miracle God did through me was the divine healing of a man that was sick unto death. He looked like a skeleton and death seemed the only option for him for he was being denied all medical treatment, due to his physical look.

God told me a week earlier about a sick man I was going to pray for. Therefore, when I reached this man, I approached him with conf - dence due to all the instructions God had given me. The power of God enveloped us and our surroundings. I started with praise and wor- ship, and then I anointed him. Before I even began to pray, the man was healed.

Two days later, the man sent me these words through a conf dant:

"Tell him (Lawrence) to hold very tightly to whoever or whatever he's serving. If it is God— he should serve him with his whole heart. The moment he stepped into the house, I felt what

I had not felt any day in my whole life—for f fty years now."

The experience I had with that man had given me conf dence in how powerful God is in every situation.

CHAPTER FOUR

THE REWARDS
IN LOVING & GIVING

Many studies in the Bible revealed that loving and giving are the two major factors that can bring even a shameful life to a glorious end.

One day, a woman told me that her problem with her husband was his "acts of giving." I asked why that was a problem. According to her, he gave even his last dime, not minding how he and his family would survive. Further, she said her husband did not feel happy when he was not giving. She said that he even gave to those that were not on good terms with him or his family. I said to her, "a giving life is a joyful life, because giving is receiving." She was a benef ciary of blessing due to her husband's giving but she could not see the benef t to her or her family, because rewards often do not announce their source.

When you give to someone you have given to God. It does not matter who or what you give, that is why it is written that we should give to others what we would have them give to us. Giving has been the source of all my life's testimonies and has taught me great lessons about the hidden blessings in giving. I do not know where I would be or what I would have become, had it not been for the rewards I received from giving. I thank God so much for the grace of giving He has given me.

I remember a time when I was in deep trouble. My friends and even my relatives failed me, even denying they ever knew me—at the time when I most needed them. Then one morning, I found my way to freedom from a book titled *"The Hidden Covenants of Blessings"*, by Dr. David O Oyedepo. I read and, for the f rst time, understood:

Blessed is he that considereth the poor:
the LORD will deliver him in time of trouble.

The LORD will preserve him, and keep him alive; and
he shall be blessed upon the earth: and thou wilt not
deliver him unto the will of his enemies.

The LORD will strengthen him upon the bed of
languishing: thou wilt make all his
bed in his sickness.
(Psalm 41:1-3)

While reading that "little giant" book, I saw a ray of light from Psalm 41. As I read it, these verses f ashed in my eyes and formed a picture which I immediately put into action, by providing school materials for all the pupils in all the elementary schools in my community.

A man came and thanked me after he saw the free books and pens his child had received. He said no government had done that in his forty-f ve years of living in that community. I am happy to inform you, to the glory of God, that Psalm 41:1-3 birthed the vision and ministry of "Covenant Seed of Restoration," which has been powerfully used in winning souls to Christ and in restoring hope in people, at all cost.

A giving life is a loving, promising, healthy and joyful life. You can give without loving but you cannot love without giving. Love, they say, is giving. When you are in love with a person, you are committed to giving to that particular person. Any love that does not involve giving is not a true love. You must give to prove your love. Your level and quality of giving show the level and quality of love you possess.

Giving moves God to action faster than prayer. Many know the testimony of father Abraham, and how he almost gave the life of his son Isaac as a sacrif ce to God. But many of us do not realize that we enjoy blessings in our lives to this day as a result of Abraham's obedience.

"And shall make him of quick understanding
in the fear of the LORD: and he shall not judge
after the sight of his eyes, neither reprove
after the hearing of his ears."
(Isaiah 11:3)

One thing our giving does is open us up for quick understanding. We read in the Bible of how God asked King Solomon what he wanted for the quality of offering he gave to God for the glory of God. A committed giver cannot run short of divine ideas because the angels are assigned to offer him whatever he needs at any time. God listens to all, but only reveals His secrets to kingdom givers.

▸ *God Gave:* God has not asked any man to do what He has not or cannot do. Many have narrowed down the word "giving" to pertain solely to fnancial exchanges. In the race of life, when times and seasons seem not to go according to the plans of God for you, even after you've prayed and fasted, there is one thing to do for a quick heavenly response to your request: give a sacrifcial offering.

One big thing I noticed when I was a young Christian was that giving is one of the weapons that bring a shortcut to long awaited blessing.

From the beginning of creation we can see how God engages in the acts of loving and giving. God made all things, gathered dust, and breathed His breath of life into that dust to create a living soul.

God never asked us to do anything without f rst demonstrating it. What separates a best friend from just a friend is the level of acts of loving and giving. "A friend indeed is a friend in need". A father in the time of need is a true father.

I met a group of inmates on one of my evangelical visits to prisons. In that group, there were two guys whose story sounded the same.

I took them through the life of Joseph, covering all he suffered in his life, even at the hand of his own relatives. I spoke of how Joseph forgave them all, even after they left him for dead in a pit.

One of the inmates said, "I will never forgive my father for the fatherly love and care he denied me." He said he had not, at any time, spoken one on one with his father, and he was twenty-five years old. His father left his mother when he was three years old and never looked back since then. He attributed all his wrongdoing to the lack of fatherly advice, love, and care he missed out on.

The second guy said he would not forgive his mother due to the role she played in the death of his father. Where there is no love, evil prevails.

"The people of the land have used oppression, and exercised robbery, and have vexed the poor and needy: yea, they have oppressed the stranger wrongfully."

(Ezekiel 22:29)

Wickedness is on the rise and increasingly spreading to every family. It is taking control of men and women, young and old, using them to commit crimes, not minding how the end looks. The devil cannot stop your blessing, but he can delay it by using you as a tool to oppress others. Greediness is at a record high in this day and age as people continue sitting on, and claiming to be personal, what belongs to the public. Watch any nation where there are great numbers of poor and needy people and you will discover there are some oppressors robbing the people of their land.

As mighty as God is, He does not oppress or rob any man of his blessings. God is a loving and giving God, even from the beginning of creation—and so He will ever be.

"For God so loved the world, that he gave his only begotten Son, that whosoever

believeth in him should not perish, but

have everlasting life."

(John 3:16)

The twenty-f ve words above are an expression of God in His loving and giving state. The verse above painted a picture of the relationship between God and man, how we—as creatures created in the image of the Creator—should love and give, because God f rst loved and gave to us. He gave His only Son as a gift and sacrif ce to free us from a pitiable, shameful life and eternal suffering and death.

For God so loved that He gave His only Son. It is your rate of loving that determines your rate of giving, "He who brings gift, brings blessings." He loved and gave! He didn't love and dance, watch or love and sing. Further, God said that whoever believed in Him would not perish, but would have eternal life. You cannot benef t from a gift until you appreciate the gift. You cannot be in love and not be in giving. Giving is profiting. He said it is more blessed to give than to receive.

"...It is more blessed to give than to receive"

(Acts 20:35).

A giving hand is always on top of the receiving hand. That is why the hand that gives is honored more than the hand that receives. Giving changes situations as no one gives to God and remains the same.

I learned this while managing a construction company as the plant manager, I had a spiritual mother to whom who I gave offerings anytime the resources of the company seemed to be running out.

There was a particular time when the company ran out of contract jobs and we started leasing machines. Not long after that, even that stopped and everybody was worried. One morning, after my daily time of praise and worship, I was touched to go and see my spiritual mother.

I arrived at her house that morning and waited patiently until she saw me and prayed for me. I gave her a very lovely offering and she blessed me all the more as she walked me to my car. I got into the car and two minutes later, my phone started ringing. While on that call, other calls where waiting. One day later, the plant yard was emptied. All the machines were gone on lease and, to the glory of God, three days later; the company won a big government contract. "Givers Never Lack."

It is lovely giving that opens the windows of heaven, through which your blessings are poured out upon you, even unto overf owing. You can wait all your life expecting your blessings, but you can give your way into the blessing of God in a single day.

► *And Peter Gave:* On a certain day, a change came upon a leader. There is a place and a day for the fulfllment of God's Word in a man's life. Enough of struggles with life, it is our heritage to be rich by the program of God for us. But fnancial fortune is a choice. When you choose what makes others rich, you are automatically rich and can be one of them.

There are countless blessings in giving. It does not matter how long you have been waiting for a turnaround in your business or relation-ship; one seed willingly sown into ministries of Jesus Christ can change your life forever.

Let us see how Jesus changed the lives of three businessmen whose lives were crippled by the devourer. This same devourer is still taking advantage of our ignorance and sitting on people's destinies, even today. Jesus Christ, during His ministry on earth, got to the lake of Gennesaret where he saw two boats standing by. The boat operators had gone to wash their nets, preparing to go home as usual.

On this day, it was business as usual for Peter and f shing partners. Peter gave use of his boat to the ministry of Jesus and that alone made Jesus love him so dearly that He changed Peter's entire life story. Jesus changed the business as usual mentality to business unusual life event and that single event changed lives that are still speaking to this day.

In the midst of frustration, Peter was kind to give his boat as seed for the ministry of Jesus.

"And Simon answering said unto him, Master, we have toiled all the night and have taken nothing; nevertheless at thy word I

will let down the net"

(Luke 5:5)

There was nothing to show for all their labors that night—a normal scene for them. Simon Peter's bank account was in the red. Perhaps his landlord was on his neck for rent and his children were out of school for not paying tuition fees. Maybe his family was hungry or had been apportioned sickness. His wife might have been preparing to go back to her parent's house. Perhaps the net seller was calling every day for his money and business was at a standstill.

The boat was Peter's only valuable asset and he relied upon it. Yet, in the midst of all his challenges and setbacks, Peter never blamed God as a reason for his failure in life.

When Jesus told him to launch out his net into the deep, I guess the f rst thought on

Peter's mind may have been, man of God, if I have given you what you wanted, please go your way and let me be.

Maybe you are a teacher, a trader, a farmer, or you and your colleagues have been in the f shing business all your lives. You may be wondering if there is any difference between where you are and the deep, where Jesus has called you. Peter was living in the hope that one day things would change for the good, but situations don't just change because one needs them to. Change comes because one works at it in the will of God. Peter knew his f nancial situation was not in line with his personal plan. He was working for change, but he was not in the will of God.

"He sent his word, and healed them,
and delivered them from their destructions."
(Psalm 107:20)

God sent His Word and delivered Peter and coworkers from pity to envy. Jesus rewrites Peter's stories, releasing his long-awaited miracles. You cannot give your money, property, time, nor services to God and remain the same. There is always a quick reaction from heaven to every investment into the Kingdom of God. It is important to know what to do when the situation seems not to go according to your expectations, and there is always something to do in order to commit God to step into the issues of your life.

► *Obedience:* You cannot benef t from one whom you choose to disobey. The difference between you and where you want to be is the order you chose not to obey. Obeying God's Word creates God's intervention, which brings into action the heavenly covenant key for a supernatural breakthrough.

You might say, "Brother Lawrence, I have observed all these things from my youth and still cannot point out to one single miracle in my life." If that is you, then one thing you lack. It is declared in Ecclesiastes.

"Let us hear the conclusion of the whole matter:

Fear God, and keep his commandments: for

this is the whole duty of man."

(Ecclesiastes 12:13)

The total duty of man is to fear God and keep His commandments. Keep up the good works you are doing. It can never be too late for God to turn your pity into envy. Mary said to the disciples of Jesus that, *"Whatever he tells you to do, do it" (John 2:5).* Complaining has not given any victim a helping hand.

Obedience was not an option for Peter— even in the midst of his frustration. Imagine if Peter had allowed his present challenges to decide whether or not he would obey the request of Jesus that day and not given Him his boat by launching out into the deep for another catch.

To obey is to be submissive to God's orders, doing whatever you are asked to do in obedience to the one in authority. To obey is to comply with any order given by one who governs you. Obedience is a choice. You can either choose to obey by complying with a given order or disobey and ignore the order.

Giving is a choice God had set for us. We have all heard the order and the benefts, but very few obey the law of giving. He said to choose to obey the law of giving into His storehouse. Then you would see God open the windows of heaven and pour out a blessing on you that you will be unable to store.

"My people are destroyed for lack of knowledge: because thou hast rejected knowledge, I will also reject thee, that thou shalt be no priest to me: seeing thou hast forgotten the law of thy God, I will also forget thy children.
(Hosea 4:6)

Does God have authority over us? Yes, He does. He is the Creator of the universe and everything therein. God controls every creature on planet earth and beyond. Jesus Christ was a man of obedience. His obedience to the order of God made him the overall man on earth. It made him the King of Kings and Lord of Lords, putting Him in command and control of every situation.

This painted a clear picture of the benefts of obedience. You cannot beneft from whatever you speak against or disobey. What manner of man is this? What they saw in Jesus and what He did, they knew was beyond the power of a natural man. Obedience is the root of faith. Whatever you obey you believe in it too. It takes a whole generation to change an obedient servant to what he believes in. God told the servants to obey all things the master ordered.

The greatest character quality of the Christian is obedience to the commandment of God. Beside Him, there is no other. When you obey the commandment of God, He gives you an express ticket to the place of favor, where you have answers to all the questions of life.

We read the story of a man called Abraham and how he was commanded by God to sacrifce his only son. When Abraham showed his obedience to the order, he became the richest man in his time (which is still speaking today).

It is prof table to obey the order from above. An obedient employee is the worker most qualif ed for promotion. An obedient child is the most loving and blessed child of his parents.

Obedience commands blessing of many colors and favor from God. Any child that obeys the voice of her parents does not fall into trouble and will never become a victim in any battle. It is a common saying that, "any f y or ant that fails to take instruction is buried with the dead."

Many folks are spending their life in prison today due to one law or another they disobeyed. Obedience pays debts and secures the life and property of a man. Obedience, it is said, quali-f es the servant to dine with the king. As an ear-ring of gold, and an ornament of f ne gold, so is a wise man with an obedient ear. To enjoy the full benef t and value of any product, you must obey the instructions for use in the manual from the manufacturer. Moses led a victorious race as a leader due to his obedience to the voice of God.

"A blessing, if ye obey the commandments of

the LORD your God, which I command

you this day."

(Deuteronomy 11:27)

Obedience gives access to many heavenly blessings. What you obey, you respect; what you respect, you love; what you love, you honor; what you honor, you fear; what you fear, you value, and; you will benef t from what you value. Obedience attracts respect everywhere everyday and is observed everywhere.

When you go to a nice restaurant and see low light, comfortably padded chairs and low music, it is a message from the management to you that you can relax, discuss matters, and feel at home as you eat and drink. But when you go to the fast food restaurant, you sit on hard plastic chairs, under bright lights, amidst loud music and talking. Their message to you

is to eat fast and move on. Give ear to orders
and obey the commands.

CHAPTER FIVE

BACK TO BASE

I grew up with the hope of living life in my own way. I thought life was so easy and full of roses, but little did I know that the journey ahead was as unpredictable as what lies in the womb of a pregnant woman. Preachers told me everything was in my command, as God promised in Deuteronomy 28:1-13, but no one ever told me what was contained in verse one,

"if thou shalt hearken diligently unto the voice

of the Lord thy God,

*to observe and to do all his commandments
which I command thee this day"
(Deuteronomy 28:1).*

▶ **The Base:** In this world of wonders, every great destiny in life begins with recognition and connections. Getting to the top depends on who you know, who backs you, and who is where you are assigned. What keeps a man's feet and voice strong is his backing, and it's that backing that gives hope for better days ahead.

When a tree is cut off from its base (its roots), it dries up. When a building shifts from its foundation, it breaks and collapses. When a man is disconnected from his base, he becomes an errand boy and a slave. In the same way, he suffers when disconnected from his source of light. Connection is what keeps two or more things in contact.

It is impossible in this world full of wonders to accomplish a dream without connections; your level of achievement depends on your level of connection. Connection is what enables two or more people to communicate effectively, not minding the distance between their destinations. A company can lose all its targeted gold if it gets disconnected from its customers for even just one day. Connection is all it takes to be known and to be on the throne.

Jesus Christ said,

"He that followeth me shall not walk in darkness, but shall have the light of life."
(John 8:12b)

Any time light is disconnected from its source, darkness takes over. Jesus came as a light to the world and lighted the world, but for any man to walk in that light, he must be connected to Jesus Christ who is the transmitter of light from heaven. He was able to shine men out of the darkness of sins with the ray of light that was upon him from heaven. Jesus Christ is a distributor of "current" to all that is connected to Him. His base has no power failure.

Every member of the Body of Christ has one particular thing, if not many things, that keep him or her very committed to Christ. One thing must move someone into either loving or hating something. It is that thing that comes to mind every time he or she feels like backing up his or her loyalty. Jesus is the one and only connection through which we can get the father's attention. That is why He promises to do whatever we ask in His name.

God is three persons in one: God the Father, God the Son and God the Holy Spirit. The Holy Spirit happens to be the closest to us, which is why anyone f lled with the Holy Spirit has express access to the throne of grace, some-thing the natural man does not have.

It can be something spiritual or some-thing physical that keeps you connected with someone. This is the reason why, when those who are committed to God are tempted to backslide, they look back and forth between their sinful past and godly present, and ulti-mately resist the temptation. As they do this, their commitment to God is strengthened.

When you are tempted, you have to ask your-self, if you back up from serving God, where and how will you get power to stand against the devil? God has made all things available to us but we still cannot access them or claim them because we are not well connected to the right source.

One other way to illustrate connection is through the operation of the wireless phone. After you purchase a wireless phone, you activate it with a service carrier. To ensure that the phone is allowed to use the network, when you dial a number using the handset, it looks for any base station around the area seeking permission to connect. The base station f rst conf rms the phone is allowed to use the network, before transmitting the call to the number you dialed. The connection is made within seconds. Because of the connection, you can talk with anyone in the world from wherever you are.

I don't know the source by which you are standing, but to those who are connected to Jesus Christ as their source, they have more than enough to be proud of. They will have peace all around and can be sure of making it to tomorrow because the grace of God (part of the connection), is upon you and more than enough for you.

"For the which cause I also suffer these things:

nevertheless I am not ashamed: for I know

whom I have believed, and am persuaded that

he is able to keep that which I have committed

unto him against that day.

Hold fast the form of sound words, which thou

hast heard of me, in faith and love

which is in Christ Jesus."

(2 Timothy 1:12-13)

You cannot love or hate what you have not tested in life. A man once said the only reason he could not serve God is because he could not give up his commitment to enjoying clubbing, drinking, smoking, and getting with all the beautiful girls in town. This is a man committed to the kingdom of the devil because he has not seen what the Kingdom of God offers.

Such a person is like the one who is fearful of quitting his current job, but gains courage to do so when he sees a better-paying job he can move to. He will not quit the kingdom of the devil until he sees better things in the Kingdom of God.

Second Timothy 1:12-13 described how the Gentiles were given their deserved portion when they dishonored their own bodies. They changed the truth of God into lies and served creatures, not the Creator. Due to their disobedience to the order of the Creator, they were given unto every unpleasant aff iction.

You may be planning how to alter one important thing that was given to you by the Creator. The good news I have for you is that you can change that plan now. Allow the Creator to handle it the way He wants it to be. If you really know the meaning and purpose of life, you will let it be.

► ***Divine Placement:*** Jesus returns in the power of the Spirit, knowing the purpose of his sonship. Jesus got to Nazareth (Base) where he was brought up. As His custom was, He went into the synagogue on the Sabbath day. As he stood up, a book was delivered unto him, by a prophet named Esaias (Isaiah)—right there in the base.

He opened the book and found this portion to read:

"The Spirit of the Lord is upon me, because he hath anointed me to preach the gospel to the poor; he hath sent me to heal the brokenhearted, to preach deliverance to the captives, and recovering of sight to the blind, to set at liberty them that are bruised"

To preach the acceptable year of the Lord (Luke 4:18-19).

After He read, Jesus closed the book, returned it to the minister in charge, and sat down. The eyes of all them that were in the synagogue were upon him. This def ned the signif cance of the fulf llment of the scriptures in their ears that day.

Every destiny is f rst built on a foundation of diff culty. No great destiny started from the place or date of birth. It takes years to build a destiny. (It can take seconds to break that many years of tireless building.) Diff culty is the ref ning f re that brings out the real color of gold from a "duty stone." Home is home.

You must face and pass the season of chaos before you can step into your season of cosmos. No good thing comes easily or by mistake. Hard times and terrible situations overcome are what qualify a man for breakthrough. No man will ever wander his way into heaven. Every man knows where he belongs because heaven is not where you found yourself. It does not ask why you are there. The atmosphere is where everyone desires to be, but you must work your way righteously into it.

► ***The Prodigal Son:*** The prodigal son, according to the parable of Jesus Christ, was a man born to and seated on wealth, before he left his throne to travel to a far country. His father had divided to him and his elder brother his inheritance (living).

The prodigal son took his portion of the wealth and goods, and went to a far country. In other words, he went on a pleasure trip. He spent all his wealth in that far country in "riotous" living. He had no plan and no savings for his time of need. (In the same way, many folks today live riotously, either knowingly and unknowingly.)

One man suffered for over f fty f ve years, working for a single company. When he retired, he took half of his pension and gratuity with him and went on a vacation—spending twenty-f ve years of benef ts in just two weeks. Can you differentiate this man from the prodigal son? No.

Riotous living is an evil attack that possesses people, just to render them useless. It takes only those in the body of Christ to live a wealthy life without been attacked by these riotous, wasteful, spiritual attacks.

The prodigal son, while he was starting his pleasure trip, never knew he would run dry any day in his life. He thought everything was going to come easily—the way he got that money from His father, but life is pregnant ("full of adversity" or "...hard work") and not full of roses.

When a person is possessed by the spirit of riotous living, he behaves as if life has no end. He is tricked into thinking he is so big and independent to do whatever comes to his mind. For the riotous man, when all is well, he can have countless friends around him, from everywhere. He never has to call them—they knock on his door because he has what they need or want. They call him honorable names and even worship him. They praise him and want to serve him, as a god, if it allows them to get a portion of his wealth. When that goes—such "friends" vanish.

"And not many days after the younger son gathered all together, and took his journey into a far country, and there wasted his substance with riotous living."
(Luke 15:13)

One morning, this guy awoke and saw a different atmosphere. He smelled a very unusual odor. He began to wonder what was wrong and then his eyes saw all that he was yet to see—there was breaking news of a mighty famine in the land, both on the radio and the television. His eyes were cleared and he attached himself to a citizen of that far country, who now hired him as a laborer and sent him into his f elds to feed swine.

Hunger became his companion. Raised with plenty, he never thought a day like this would ever come to his life. He was hungry, dirty, and so poor he even slept among the pigs—even trying to eat their food.

There is a saying, "Givers never lack," that I know to be true. Only givers who give in the wisdom of God remain in plenty because it is more blessed to give than to receive.

Think of that man that took all his pension money and traveled to a far country for pleasure. Such a man has no future or vision for himself. A vacation is a time reasonable people use to relax, to birth ideas, and to search out solution to problems their frazzled lives have not allowed them. Others, like this man, used his vacation time as a time of pleasure-seeking, to party, and to drink in a way they aren't able to due to the pressure of the kind of job they do.

"He that gathereth in summer is a wise son:

but he that sleepeth in harvest is a son

that causeth shame.

Blessings are upon the head of the just:

but violence covereth the mouth of the wicked."

(Proverbs 10:5-6)

The only time they would have used to rest the body is the time they used "over labor" the body in the name of vacation trip—one that tripped them into lack. All that the prodigal son went through is still happening in the lives of countless people these days. When there is plenty, they give no thought to the days ahead.

"And when he came to himself, he said, How many hired servants of my father's have bread enough and to spare, and I perish with hunger!"

(Luke 15:17)

The prodigal son came to his senses. He arose and walked back home to ask his father for forgiveness. But the father was not holding his past against his son.

The prodigal son even planned to condemn himself before his father, to express that he was no longer worthy to be called his son. But as soon as his father saw his son, he welcomed him greatly and ordered the servants to dress him with the best robe, ring, and shoes. He called for celebration and restored his son who had returned. He turned a King when he got to his base. There is no place like home they say.

His father said, "My son was dead, and he is alive again." His son was absent from home for a long time. Perhaps his father had given him up for dead—surely he had walked the path of death.

When the eldest brother returned from working in the f eld, he heard the sound of music from afar, got home and saw people dancing. This looked very strange to him because he knew of no planned party when he left home to work the morning of that fateful day.

He wondered at what he saw and asked one of the servants what was going on. He was told that his younger brother had returned home from a riotous journey. With all the eldest brother saw and heard from the servant, he became angry. He complained to his father— why had such a party never been thrown for him? He had been faithful to his father. The good, loving father told him that everything was his, but now that they had found one of them that was lost, they must welcome and rejoice with him.

"Either what man having one hundred sheep, if he loses one doth not go and f nd it diligently till he f nds it?, (Luke 15:4) And when he has found it he called friends and neighbors together, saying rejoice with me for I have found one of my sheep that was missing" The remaining ninety-nine sheep are quite a lot to keep up with, but love causes you to feel bad when missing even one of them. At a time like this, people may come to eat and dance with you, but not all of them will be happy for you in recovering your lost property—even those closed to you (like relatives).

"Behold, I stand at the door, and knock: if any man hear my voice, and open the door, I will come in to him, and will sup with him, and he with me."

(Revelation 3:20)

In the same way, Jesus is ready to receive any lost soul into the Kingdom of God. He knows those that have lost their hope in God and those who cannot wait for the appointed time; deciding to try something else for survival. The good news is, no place is like home.

God knows all your needs, including the need to open up for him. God has no problem blessing you more than you expect. He only needs time to grow you up so you can contain that which He has for you. He is a loving father who does not want any of his children to go astray. He cares deeply about each of his children's future. He promises to be with you. Even when adversity comes like a f ood, he said it shall not overf ow you. The f ery trials shall not burn or consume you.

> *"My people hath been lost sheep: their*
> *shepherds have caused them to go astray, they*
> *have turned them away on the mountains:*
> *they have gone from mountain to hill, they have*
> *forgotten their resting place."*
> *(Jeremiah 50:6)*

▸ ***Be Born Again:*** Folks, I don't know which area of your life has grown from a hill to a mountain. (There is a huge difference between overcoming hills versus mountains.) The good news I have for you is that Jesus is ever ready to receive you into your place of rest; a place of eternal life where you will enjoy all the Kingdom resources.

You might say to me that your sins are beyond pardon. That is a lie. It does not matter how far you have fallen into sin. The price has been paid in full on the cross through the blood of Jesus Christ, and no single debt is paid twice. The moment you open up to Jesus, he will step in and change your entire past to a brand new beginning where no one will recall your yesterday.

Many have remained where they are for the fear of the high level of sins they have been involved in. Everybody in the Body of Christ has a "past" marred by grievous sin, but the good news is that there is no recall of the past in the Kingdom of God.

"Therefore if any man be in Christ, he is a new creature: old things are passed away; behold, all things are become new."

(2 Corinthian 5:17)

You are completely new. No record of your past exists. Your body and hair color may look the same as it used to, but you have been transformed into a new creature. Your speech is now changed due to the change of your mindset. Jesus has now taken over your life's affairs. Your family background now has no hold on you anymore. Whatever trace of disease or untimely death in your family is no longer your portion. Your blood has been transfused with the blood of Christ. Becoming a new creature affects every area of your life. Your f rst and last name may remain the same, but—good news—you now belong to the family of Christ, which is now your base.

Your acceptance of Christ has changed your life and made you a citizen of heaven. It has also cut you off from all the unclean spirits from your forefathers. What your non-Christian relatives may suffer will never come near you.

"But as many as received him, to them gave

he power to become the sons of God, even to

them that believe on his name:

Which were born, not of blood, nor of the will of

the f esh, nor of the will of man, but of God."

(John 1:12-13)

No man can parade around with a U.S. passport without being a citizen of the U.S., and no man can claim to be a citizen of America without having proof to prove his claims. What qualif es you as a customer of a bank is the checkbook or check card bearing your account number—not the money in the bank. You can have a checkbook with a zero balance and still be a "customer" of a bank.

"And these signs shall follow them that believe;

In my name shall they cast out devils; they

shall speak with new tongues."

(Mark 16:17)

When a man is born again, he's given an identity that identifes him as a citizen of the Kingdom of God. The identity gives him access to Kingdom resources at all time, at any location. The f rst access given to man at rebirth is access to the power and authority of the name of Jesus Christ. Without the citizen identity you can call out the name of Jesus a thousand times and still, nothing happens. Your call goes nowhere if you are not born again. I am always happy when Jesus said "verily, verily" because I know he's directing it to everyone. I must be born again to live again in the Kingdom of God.

New birth is the only way to obtain a direct visa into the Kingdom where you can be redeemed for the throne of glory as a queen, princess, prince, and priest. The name of Jesus is the f rst thing we are identifying with as a Kingdom priest at new birth. The wonders in the name sneaked life to everyone.

CHAPTER SIX

THE POWER OF FOCUS

Focus is the only way to a successful life journey. When a man is focused, he thinks of the end from the beginning. That enables him to correct whatever could have been a stumbling block or an obstacle on his way.

Every day, many argue that life cannot be described as a journey, that instead, life should be described as a process. Life is a journey.

Picture ten students beginning their four years of college together, but in the end, only three graduated with a degree. What happened to the rest? They were taken away by the storms of life.

Picture a family of six, where only two live to celebrate their f ftieth birthday. Not everyone that starts a journey will make it to the end. But there is a formula put in place by the Creator that secures life to the fullest, if properly applied.

There are six heavenly weapons (formulas) to put in place for a successful journey of life.

▶ *The Weapon of the Word of God*

My son, attend to my words; incline thine ear unto my sayings.

Let them not depart from thine eyes; keep them in the midst of thine heart.

For they are life unto those that f nd them, and health to all their f esh

Keep thy heart with all diligence; for out of it

are the issues of life.

Put away from thee a froward mouth, and

perverse lips put far from thee.

(Proverbs 4:20-24)

The Word of God is the manual or instructions given by God, the Creator of life, for how people are to live life. The Word of God is the power of God, the eyes of God, and the action and manifestation of God. The Word of God gives the angels orders to act upon, serving as the mouth of God in action. The Word of God is the commandment of God and the covenant of God. The Word of God is the image, light, knowledge and wisdom of God.

When a man is not walking in His God-given way into the unknown, the only thing that can deliver him back to his rightful path is the Word of God. It is the Word of God that leads the way out of hopelessness to hopefulness. The Word of God brings the expression of the power and promise of God into action in our lives.

The angels assigned to us will do nothing without the Word of God from our mouths. The Word of God is the weapon God has placed in the hands of every man to overcome his ene-mies to be on the winning side. The Word of God reveals the end of the journey of life.

The light of God shines on the path of man through the Word of God and the declaration of the Word puts the favor of God into action. The difference between where you are and where you want to be is the level of the knowledge of the Word of God in you.

The Word of God is the only key to increasing our faith in God. It is the seed of faith in our lives. Show me a man of faith and I will show you the seat of the Word of God. It is the Word of God that gives birth to faith and faith that brings the Word of God alive and into action. Any man without the knowledge of God is like a package without the destination address, the package belongs to nobody.

It is the Word that delivers a man from darkness to light and from the kingdom of Satan to the Kingdom of God. The Word guides man to his inheritance. Constant feeding on the Word giveth life and health to all our f esh. The Hebrew word for "health" means "medicine to our f esh." God has not programmed any form of medication to be taken when sickness comes to our f esh. All He gave to us as a cure to our pain and sickness is the weapon of the Word. The more doses of the Word you take in and apply to your life, the healthier and longer you will live and prosper.

God tells us to declare the Word against whatever wants to deny His will in our lives. If you can say to that problem part of your life what is written in the Word against it, the Bible says it must bow to the Word. You don't need physical power or wealth to be healed—not even the help of a human being.

The Word is the Spirit of God that giveth life and health.

"It is the spirit that quickeneth; the esh
prof teth nothing: the words that I speak unto
you, they are spirit, and they are life".
(John 6:63)

The Word of God has the power to heal anyone that believes in it. It can also deliver believers from destruction. The Bible said;

"Jesus saith unto him, Go thy way; thy son

liveth, And the man believed the word that

Jesus had spoken unto him, and

he went his way"

(John 4:50)

This man must have witnessed the unveiling powers contained in the Word and boldly believed in Jesus, speaking the Word only. That was faith in action on the part of the centurion. He knew the Word was as active as Jesus Himself; the Word was all he needed to deliver his servant from the evil attack. I pray the Word you are feeding on now will set you free from evil attacks in Jesus' name. The Word of God reveals the will and plan of God for man. It shows the picture of God to him who f nds it. "There is no recovery without discovery, however". When a man f nds the Word of God, he obtains the ability to control every circumstance of life.

> *"Call unto me, and I will answer thee, and*
> *show thee great and mighty things,*
> *which thou knowest not."*
> *(Jeremiah 33:3)*

"Call unto me" in other words means, "speak my words, and remind me of my words." When you speak God's Word, He will not only answer you, but He will show you great and wondrous things which you and your family lines knew not. When you speak the Word, you remind God of His covenant with father Abraham. The confession of the Word turns every situation and season in life to your advantage and positions you for the establishment of God's divine purpose in you. The Word keeps man focused on his path to destiny.

"In the beginning was the Word, and the Word was with God, and the Word was God."

(John 1:1)

The Word of God is God Himself. He created the world in the beginning and all the inhabitants therein by His Word. He holds sit up by the power of His Word. There is power in the Word of God.

Any man or woman who is well-equipped with the weapon of the Word can also create his own world through faith and be able to stand by it. The Word of God is ever current for the successful operation of man's dominion on planet earth. You must have the understanding that the Bible was written by men who were inspired by God through the Holy Spirit: The LORD revealed Himself through His Word.

The truth of God is in His Word as are the ways of God. There is no better tomorrow without the Word. All you need in your time of trouble or joy is the Word of God. Just one Word of God can better your life forever. Go in search of the Word and focus on it. It is all you need to get there.

Whenever you are in need of information about a product, you go to the manufacture's manual or website to check for the right information because he who produced it knows all about it. In the same way, you need the Bible for the preservation of your life, whether it be for health, prosperity, favor, protection—you name it! It is all there for you in the Word.

Job said when the candle (Word) of God shined upon his head, by His light he walked through darkness. Go in search of wisdom to solve that particular problem you are facing. The word of God will be a f re to guide your way. Your limitation is a result of your lack of the Word. When you are full of the Word, you will never miss the knowledge you need again in Jesus' name, Amen.

▸ ***The Weapon of Faith***: The process of transformation from being in a pitiable situation to an enviable position as a king begins with the formation of faith, by the knowledge of the Word of God. The knowledge of the word of God tells us to confess whatever we need before it can be delivered into our hands. "Whatever is too big in our mouth is equally too big in our hands".

There is no output without input and no harvest season without a planting season. There is no receiving in the kingdom of heaven without applying the laws of asking, believing, and acting. Faith is the beauty of Christianity, as nothing works without faith.

"For verily I say unto you, That whosoever shall
say unto this mountain,
Be thou removed, and be thou cast into the
sea; and shall not doubt in his heart, but shall
believe that those things which he saith shall
come to pass; he shall have
whatsoever he saith."
(Mark 11:23)

Your destiny comes to reality the moment you start confessing with your mouth and believing with your heart. Faith is the mother of saying it, doing it, receiving it, and telling it to others. Faith is a mountain-mover. Faith is the healing balm booster, as prescribed by the great physician, Jesus Christ. Faith is the many-a-day every man or woman needs to keep their systems the way they should be. Faith does not answer "no" to any questions of life and has no closed door in the affairs of life.

Faith is the weapon that keeps life as designed by the Creator.

What is-and why Faith?

"Now faith is the substance of things hoped for, the evidence of things not seen."

(Hebrew 11:1)

Now think of the money you have deposited in your bank account. The account has your name, social security number, drivers' license number, address, and signature attached to it—all the information you were asked to provide. Not just anyone can conduct a transaction on your account. Your bank identity or checking account card gives you legal access to cash money from your account. Even when you show up to get money from your account, you will still be asked for your checking account card. No matter what your level of investment is in the bank, if you try to get money from your account without your legal access card, your request will be denied.

"the substance of things hoped for,

the evidence of things not seen"

(Hebrews 11:1).

You cannot see it, nor handle it, but you believe it exists. Seeing it before believing it is not faith. Probability is not in the operation of faith. Faith is "I can do" and trust is a child of faith.

The f rst part of training as a pilot is in how to trust all the gauges and instruments on the airplane. No matter how high the plane f ies, the pilot cannot feel threatened. The passengers sit conf dently on airplane f ights out of belief in the operational skills of the pilot. Even when passengers cannot see the direction of the plane, they still believe they are on the right route.

Life has no meaning outside of faith. God has given to all men all that He promised. But all men must apply the weapons of faith to actualize it or what has been given will be ineffective. The Bible def nition of faith implies that putting the Word of God into action is the only way of committing Him to perform what He promises.

"And blessed is she that believed: for there

shall be a performance of those things which

were told her from the Lord."

(Luke 1:45)

Faith empowers your spiritual performance with God and gives you a meaningful life. Life has no future without the application of faith to make the journey smooth.

Faith does not just believe anything. Believing is acting on the application, operation and expression of conf dence in God's Word. It is the faithful intake and practice of Scripture that creates a great and promising future.

"So then faith cometh by hearing,
and hearing by the word of God"
(Romans 10:17).

It takes the continual hearing of the Word of God to birth and nurture faith. Faith is located in the heart of man. It is conceived by the revelation of the Word, nurtured by concentration on the truth and birthed by dedication to life.

"And he said unto her, Daughter,
be of good comfort:

thy faith hath made thee whole;

go in peace."

(Luke 8:48)

Faith works when backed by determination. The woman with the issue of blood for twelve years was made whole in a few seconds as a result of her determination to f nd freedom from her aff iction. Faith without action is dead. Faith is not making God responsible for our situation, but acting on the Word to perform miracles. God will not move until you f rst move in faith.

▶ *The Weapon of Faith & Hope*: These are two different words that have close meaning, but two different directions. Faith is def ned as the substance of things hoped for, the evidence of things not seen, but hope is the expression of desire. Many are living by hope, but very few are living in faith. It is faith that gives value to hope.

In the journey of life, it is impossible to accomplish anything good without the application of faith.

"Now faith is the substance of things hoped for, the evidence of things not seen."

(Hebrews 11:1)

Faith is the power by which the desires of life are possessed. Faith can be seen as more than the sum total of trust, belief, conf dence, hope and mental ideas. Hope grows from faith, which is why it is frustrating to live life without hope that is birthed by faith. Faith is the mechanism that causes what is not into existence. There is no gold without faith and it is impossible to possess the spirit of faith without having gold to show for it. A life without hope is a life of hopelessness which has no bearing.

There is a dead hope and a living or lively hope. Hope is what keeps life steady on the runway of life. Hope is for tomorrow's event, while faith is for the now happening.

Hope can be classif ed as a mental idea that operates on future events. Hope is an image of the mind. No wonder they say, "Where there is hope there is life," because hope always presents a picture as "if today is a failure, tomorrow might be a success."

"For to him that is joined to all the living there is hope: for a living dog is better than a dead lion."
(Ecclesiastes 9:4)

Again, when there is life, there is hope. Hope never stops acting until it sees the end of the matter. As mighty as the lion may be compared to other animals, and the dog in particular, did you know that once the lion is dead it is as useless as nothing? "A living dog is better than a dead lion," because the living is still in action and hopeful, but the dead is useless, an empty vessel in which nothing can be found.

Hope to life is powerful but should not be confused with faith. Some say words in their season of pity like, "I hope tomorrow will bring a better result" or, "I hope the end will be successful." Faith is birthed and nurtured by the Word of God, while hope is birthed by the imagination of human intellect. Hope facilitates the f ow of faith that makes things happen for good.

Hope relies on expectation, while Faith is always in action, bringing the Word of God into manifestation. The story of the three f shermen in the Bible tells us how they lived, surviving hardship in the name of hope. That was not the f rst night of failure in their f shing careers. All the years previous had been business as usual. (Living as a success is not for all.)

The day faith came on the scene, their story changed overnight. Jesus spoke faith into action and wonder was the order of the day. Eyes couldn't believe what they saw. A life without faith is a life without hope, and a life without faith and hope is a life without proofs.

▶ *The Weapon of Fasting & Prayer*: Another weapon God made available for turning a pitiable life into an enviable one is the weapon of fasting and prayer.

Prayer is a two-way communication between God the Creator and man the creature. It does not go one way, because a one-way prayer is a prayer that does not get the attention of God. The sense of prayer is all about getting heavenly intervention to change situations by transforming shame into glory. Show me a truly prayerful man and I will show you a war-winning man.

The apostolic ministry was also known as a prayerful ministry, built on the foundation of prayer. When you think of spiritual warfare, you think of prayer, of mountain-moving prayer, and you think of getting God's attention for divine empowerment. Think of prayer.

"Call unto me, and I will answer thee, and show thee great and mighty things, which thou knowest not."

(Jeremiah 33:3)

When we call heaven for help, we do not only get answers to what we called for, but more things are unveiled for us and prayers answered. Why? Because the one seated in heaven knows all we need to stand.

Prayer works miracles for them that pray and bring to pass great and mighty things, by the manifestation of God's will in man. Prayer reveals the secret of success in the Kingdom of God to those who have the ability to fast and pray.

"Ask of me, and I shall give thee the heathen for thine inheritance, and the uttermost parts of the earth for thy possession."

(Psalm 2:8)

"Ask of Me and I shall give thee," is the one condition God puts in the advancement and victory of His cause. Conquerors don't quit in prayer, because prayer is the only way of spiritual refreshment for the battles that lie ahead.

When something is not what it seems, there is a strong force in operation. After creation, God saw everything and behold, it was very good. So anything that is not very good is the f nger of the enemy in operation.

God deals with every man according to His emotional expression in prayer. There is no receiving without f rst asking the one that owns all that you need or want. Every receiving is birthed by asking. To get to know new places demands moving from the old place to the new place. To get new things demands asking for them.

The disciples of Jesus Christ learned that the connection which brings together God the Father, God the Son, and God the Holy Spirit, is prayer. Jesus was a master in prayer and it was one of his strongest weapons in battle against the enemy. When people pray for an issue, changes are bound to occur.

Many are living in spiritual darkness and have no clue of the right way to be made free. It is true that every man passes through one form of life or the other, but very few become victorious at the end. The secrets of the Kingdom of God are made known only to those that faithfully fast and pray.

Why fasting and prayer? Because these are all we need to locate our divine place. In fasting and prayer, the spirit man is strengthened to overcome spiritual forces. When things seem not be going as promised by God, apply the weapon of fasting and prayer.

► *The Weapon of the Tongue:* It is true that no man has ever grown past the words of his mouth because what he says is what he is and what he gets.

Earlier we saw how, from the creation of the world, God speaks words into action by saying what should and should not be. Behold, they came to be and were shaped and formed according to His spoken words. We are serving a speaking God who expects us to speak our victories into action.

"Death and life are in the power of the tongue: and they that love it shall eat the fruit thereof."

(Proverbs 18:21)

A man's life is solely dependent upon his confessions, and we are all judged by them. Your feelings cannot manifest until you start speaking out words that birth your actions. He who keeps his mouth keeps his life because, "Death and life are in the power of the tongue." If you can control your speech you can also control the direction of your life.

Speaking is part of life, a major characteristic of human beings, but that speaking can also render us a non-living being for those that cannot be quiet.

You cannot speak pitifully and be envied. You cannot speak good health and become sick. And you cannot speak peace and get into trouble. If you can talk your way into prison, in the same way, you can talk yourself out of prison. This is why drug addicts always get into heavy trouble when they are under the infuence of drugs.

You can, in a way, deny what you smell or see, but it is very diff cult to deny what you say because the sound and vibration stand as evidence by which you are judged. If you can correctly account for your words, you can also account for your actions. Your words form your belief and your belief is responsible for your relationships with people around you.

God said that if you can speak to that giant mountain in your life to be moved and cast into the sea, believing in your heart the words you speak, it will be done as you have spoken.

"For verily I say unto you, That whosoever shall

say unto this mountain,

Be thou removed, and be thou cast into the

sea; and shall not doubt in his heart, but shall

believe that those things (words) which he saith

shall come to pass; he shall have

whatsoever he saith."

(Mark 11:23)

Start making a difference in your life today by speaking words of blessings and testimonies into your life, and before long, things will start changing for the better. What form of giant do you have in your life today that is not letting you experience the promises of God to the full? It is time you identify that giant and start addressing it with your given weapons. The angels act on whatever comes out of your mouth, but you must speak them into action.

King Solomon wrote that there is a time to speak and a time to be quiet. Don't say the right thing at the wrong time, for there is *"...a time to keep silence, and a time to speak"* (Ecclesiastes 3:7)

The right word, coming out of your mouth at the wrong time, is as dangerous as committing crime with your hands. With your tongue you can condemn any other tongue that rises against you, by speaking death to anything that wants you dead and speaking life to anything that wants you alive.

Your tongue is a warring weapon God gave you for defense against your enemies. Use it well because you can be a victim of the weapon in your hand if you lack the proper knowledge of its usage.

► *The Weapons of Forgiveness:* Everyone that carries the spirit of forgiveness dwells in God; this is a heavenly virtue. There is no freedom for a man without the spirit of forgiveness at work in him. Bitterness and un-forgiveness is a disease the devil uses to afflict people. If the devil can stop you from forgiving, he also denies you of your covenant rights.

"But if ye forgive not men their trespasses,

neither will your Father forgive

your trespasses"

(Matthew 6:15).

Un-forgiveness is an impenetrable bar-rier which hinders most would-be answered prayers. Forgiveness should be a "must" for everyone in the Body of Christ, because it pays off to live in a life of forgiveness. Without the spirit of forgiveness in a man, the redemption of Jesus will not have any bearing on him.

If what people say has no grounds in your life, they cannot stop you from stepping into your destiny. Give no thought to their words. You don't become what they say until you start thinking about and believing what they say. Let go of the past and focus your attention on what awaits you ahead. Go past the bridge and get on the freeway.

CHAPTER SEVEN

The Power of Confidence

Every great achievement in life is packaged in the mysteries of confidence. It is only the high-rise mansion, seated on the foundation of confidence that becomes victorious and enviable. The greatest word anyone loves to hear from another is that they have a high level of confidence in him or her. You cannot have confidence in yourself in anything and still become a failure in it.

What is and why confidence? Confidence is simply the belief in someone or something to be right. It could also be defined as the feeling

that someone or something is true and will pro-
duce a rewarding result.

Faith is another good friend of conf dence.
Faith is the only force that can put God's
Word into action. Confidence is the foundation whereby faith stands. Having confidence
in God; that He is able to do all He promised,
is what helps a believer to stand strong in faith.
God has done His part by laying down for us
the fundamental rules to be observed for us to
walk in His unlimited blessing.

If I was to say there is no different between
Bible faith and Bible confidence, many would
wonder what I mean. But rather than confuse
the issue, let me unveil some hidden mysteries
concerning confidence in God.

Confidence is strengthened by focusing on
the good days; what and what you have faced in
life and survived. You cannot build confidence

by thinking about all the failures you have had in life, or of how "mean" God is being to you.

You may have faith as big as the globe, but without conf dence you cannot qualify for any blessing from God. Be conf dent in your-self to survive this life no matter what you are facing. Achieving your goal in life is not a result of struggle, but a result of believing in yourself that, you will be there one day, no matter what.

Hard work is rewarding but when hard work lacks conf dence it becomes hard failure. Stop wasting your precious time thinking about what you are seeing and how you are feeling; medi-tate on what God has said about you. When you conf dently believe in your heart and start confessing that belief, God will deliver all bless-ings into your hand.

"For as he thinketh in his heart, so is he" *(Proverbs 23:7).* You cannot grow taller than the thoughts of your mind. What you think is

what you are in life. You cannot think like a pitiful man and be victorious. It is your thinking that forms your level of confidence in any situation.

Confidence is the spiritual force that shows you the way of hard work which receives reward. No man was born with a "success label" on his face. Every man came to this life the same way and it does not matter how young or old you have been around. Some work with confidence to succeed in life, while others work without confidence to follow whichever way life goes.

"And without all contradiction the less is
blessed of the better."
(Hebrews 7:7)

Success offers no advantage due to age. Believing in yourself qualifes you as a candidate for success. When you believe and work in the commands of God, you become what He said about you.

As others go around complaining about what they don't have to succeed in life, others are building confidence in God to use the little they have to succeed and get what they need. Those who waver don't get any further than where they are. Only those who hold fast the profession of their conf dence in God will walk in the light of heaven.

Cast not away therefore your confidence,

which hath great recompence of reward.

(Hebrews 10:35)

No soldier dies in the front lines of war without first running out of confidence in the weapons he carries. It was the confidence David had in God that moved him to face and defeated the mighty Goliath. When a man in war loses conf -

dence in himself, before long, he will become a casualty, because once conf dence is gone out of a man, anything can defeat him. In whatever you do, one thing you must f ght to protect is your conf dence.

> *"Also I heard the voice of the Lord, saying,*
> *Whom shall I send, and who will go for us?*
> *Then said I, Here am I; send me."*
> *(Isaiah 6:8)*

Jesus Christ was a man of conf dence. He was so conf dent in Himself to accomplish His mission and so believed God would back him up, that He was ready to face any mountain that came His way. Righteousness is not just about observing the laws of Moses, but is also about having conf dence in God that He is faithful and will do all what He promised.

The conf dence Jesus had in God brought Lazarus back to life with a single command Jesus gave. I don't know in what position of life you have been in or if you are defeated as a result of doubt. But one thing I know that you must know is that your failure is affecting thousands of people who have been assigned to you as the one through whom they will accomplish their destinies. All you need is to look for one scripture in the Bible that addresses your situation and develop your conf dence in it.

"Teaching them to observe all things
whatsoever I have commanded you:
and, lo, I am with you always, even unto the
end of the world. Amen."
(Matthew 28:20)

This is a promise to hold on to, when Jesus says He is with you always, He meant what

He said—even unto the end of the world. He's got your back "until death do you part." If He has said it and has done it for someone else, expect Him to do the same for you.

The woman with the issue of blood confidently broke every security protocol to touch Jesus because her confidence in the healing power of Jesus was at record high. The confident in your heart is what powers up the weapon of faith to perform wonders. God is still God. Start building up your confidence in the power of God today. Become an "I can do it" person. By doing this, you will guarantee success in all your endeavors.

"Whosoever shall say unto this mountain, Be thou removed, and be thou cast into the sea; and shall not doubt in his heart, but shall believe that those

things which he saith shall come to pass; he shall have whatsoever he saith."
(Mark 11:23)

Faith in God denotes confidence in God. Many understand the act of having conf dence in someone, but very few can truly def ne what faith is all about. When you are confident in someone, it will take the whole world to talk you into doubting that person, who they are, or what they can do.

Speaking to a mountain requires confidence in who you are and what you believe in. You cannot address a mountain with fear and doubt all over you. When your confidence is mixed with faith, you turn your world into one of miracles and wonders. "I can do it" always make it to the f nish line. It is the confidence in your heart that turns on the "I can do it" in you. You don't get defeated until you lose confidence in your ability to succeed. You cannot confess anything positive if your confidence is gone or down.

"Finally, my brethren, be strong in the Lord, and in the power of his might."

(Ephesians 6:10)

To be strong in the Lord is to be confident in the Word of the Lord. It is confidence that provokes faith to turn negative situations into positive situations. Our confessions have so much to do with our lives. We spend all day talking about our feelings rather than focusing on the promises of God for us.

Abraham could not receive the blessings of God for him until he was confident that God, who had made the promises to him, was faithful. When His confidence in God became strong, His confession changed. His confidence and confession delivered into his hands, the long-awaited blessings of God.

There is no mountain you cannot climb if you can take a moment to build up conf dence in yourself. A confident messenger is the only servant that becomes the successor of the boss when his journey is dawn. If you are in need of healing, conf dence in God's healing power is all you need. If you need a child, start confessing yourself into being a mother or father of many. Before long you will have more than you can imagine.

Jesus Christ is more than enough to them that conf dently confess Him as their healer and their deliverer. When you conf dently confess Jesus as your husband, He gives you all the protection a husband can give to his wife.

When you conf dently confess Jesus as your employer, he gives you the best paying job you can imagine. To them that conf dently confess

Jesus as their leader, He leads them to the right places, the right people, and the right path to follow. I believe God that from now on you will never be the same person you were before reading this book. In Jesus' name. Amen.

CHAPTER EIGHT

A Life from Pity to Envy

There are some folks around that are naturally diffcult to deal with. No matter what
you do to please them and play soft, they only
seem to harden up their minds more and more
on you. One of the main reasons great men
fall so sharply from honor to shame is due to
attacks which result from something they did to
someone years back, perhaps someone they
work or do business with.

Your spouse can pose a very complicated
threat to you sometimes. Even someone you
are meeting for the frst time or to whom you

are rendering help can leave you a victim. Many have been trapped in attacks in the name of helping someone. Though some of these even saw a way out of their trapped situations, but they chose to stay and see it to the end.

▶ *Love:* Love is one of the weapons we can use to secure a promising destiny. Where there is love, there is peace and understanding. Love does not keep records of faults or wrongdoing of any kind. Love does not run out of patience, no matter the situation. Love is a patient dog that eats the fattest bones.

"Set me as a seal upon thine heart, as a seal

upon thine arm: for love is strong as death;

jealousy is cruel as the grave:

the coals thereof are coals of fre, which

hath a most vehement fame."

(Song of Solomon 8:6)

Love is as strong as death. No wonder they say marriage is, "For better or worse". Love is love because it does not have a second thought. Love gives rest in all situations. Those whose lives have no love; they are always stressed when faced with situations. Love burns like a high f ame of gas that no water can quench, nor f ood drown.

The regrets of love always come at last— after the "I-do's" have been done. Love sees no threat ahead. It costs nothing materially to have a natural love, but it costs much more to stir up hatred. Only those who love you for who and what you are will stay with you through your tough times. Those who will not be there to help you in your downfall are those who loved you for what you had, not for who you are.

"I drew them with cords of a man, with bands

of love: and I was to them

as they that take off the yoke on their jaws, and

I laid meat unto them"

(Hosea 11:4).

Love is the only force that can lift a man up from the foor of pity to the throne of envy because love stirs up the favor of God. You must possess the force of true love to be identifed among men as a man to envy. Only the power of love can single you out for greatness in the midst of failure.

Love is a choice. You can choose to love or to hate, but remember there is no peace or security without love. When you are out of love, you are in for fear. No matter what situation you fnd yourself in, choose to be in love with everyone around you.

▶ ***The Love and Fear of God:*** The fear of the Lord is the beginning of wisdom, King

Solomon wrote. Anywhere you see wisdom; greatness is at the corner of it, if not the pillar. The love and fear of the Lord is what tells you what to do and what not to do. It guides and directs you to the path of greatness. There is a good reason to be kind and to show kindness to others, even when you don't feel like being kind. Something inside tells you to be kind because there is profit in kindness. "The world is a small place," they say. You never knew the world to be a small place until you see what you least expected.

"And be ye kind one to another, tenderhearted,

forgiving one another, even as God for Christ

sake hath forgiven you."

(Ephesians 4:32)

We saw a good account of the rewards of those who show kindness to others, even to those who seem to be difficult. You can never fail in life as long as you remain kind towards others; you are never more like Jesus than when you are walking with others in kindness.

The story of Joseph had always been my only hope in life whenever I am in a difficult situation. I hope this will help you also to fix your focus on your destiny (even if broken).

At the age of seventeen, Joseph started sharing with his brethren the dreams he had about his destiny. The moment the devil heard of his dream, he turned Joseph's brothers against him and Joseph found himself in the middle of a storm he never saw coming.

The love and fear Joseph had for God was his only secret for winning the battle that paved the way for his transformation from being pitiful to being envied. As his brothers saw him growing like a palm tree, they began to break their silence and they hated him all the more for his dreams, as well as his words.

"And his brethren said to him, Shalt thou
indeed reign over us?
or shalt thou indeed have dominion over
us? And they hated him yet the more for his
dreams, and for his words.

And he dreamed yet another dream, told it to
his brethren, and said, Behold, I have dreamed
a dream more; and, behold, the sun and the
moon and eleven stars made
obeisance to me."
(Genesis 37:8-9)

His father was threatened by his dream as well as his brothers, when Joseph told them another dream he had dreamt. His brethren were filled with hatred and envy; not pity, because his focus was above theirs. They planned to kill Joseph to end his dreams. It is best to be mindful of whom you tell your dream. He might not want you to fulf ll that dream.

They met over and over to decide how to get rid of both Joseph and his dream.

"Come now therefore, and let us slay him, and cast him into some pit, and we will say, Some evil beast hath devoured him: and we shall see what will become of his dreams.

And Reuben heard it, and he delivered him out of their hands; and said, Let us not kill him.

And Reuben said unto them, Shed no blood, but cast him into this pit that is in the wilderness, and lay no hand upon him; that he might rid him out of their hands, to deliver him to his father again".

(Genesis 37:20-22)

God delivered Joseph through Reuben. They sold Joseph as a slave. But Joseph, in all this, didn't give up because he knew what awaited him. After selling Joseph, his brethren thought they had accomplished their plan to end his enviable destiny.

▸ *Joseph became a Pity:* The Bible states that "Joseph was sold to- and became a slave to Potiphar, who was a senior army off cer of Pharaoh's in Egypt"

"And the Midianites sold him into Egypt unto Potiphar, an off cer of Pharaoh's, and captain of the guard"

(Genesis 37:36).

It is never a "piece of cake" to gain anything precious. The times and seasons Joseph
endured helped him and trained Him for the
greater days ahead. Through it all, favor still followed Joseph, even into a strange land where
everything worked in his favor.

Life in a world of wonder made Potiphar
love Joseph. He put Joseph in command of
everybody and all the property in his house
except his wife. Still, the devil never gets tired
of attacks. He kept pressing further to end
Joseph's dream.

As if slavery wasn't bad enough for the devil,
he still used Potiphar's wife to test Joseph with
sex. One cool day, Joseph was left alone at
home with Potiphar's wife. The woman, with
her idle and blinded mind controlled by an evil
spirit, held Joseph and dragged him to have
sex with her, but Joseph refused the sinful offer
and ran away! In order not avoid staining his

relationship with God; Joseph rejected the devil's offer to have sex with his master's wife.

She then shouted, "Rape, Rape!" and lied to her husband about how Joseph tried to rape her, but Joseph, with the hope that his loving master would not believe her stories, waited to see his reaction. Sadly, Joseph was arrested, without proper investigation, and became a prisoner for an offense he didn't commit. A man of dreams (envy) became a man of pity.

Nevertheless, while in prison, his dream was still manifesting. Despite all the hurdles Joseph was facing, he became a star even in prison because the favor of God was with him.

Joseph became a "miracle" slave and was appointed the head of prison administration. There in the prison, he met two friends, former workers for Pharaoh. They had a dream and Joseph interpreted it for them. It came to pass just as he had interpreted it. Sometime later, they were released from prison and given back their duty posts in Pharaoh's palace, but they forgot all about their friend Joseph for many years.

Then one night Pharaoh had a terrible dream and there was nobody to interpret the dream for him. He was very concerned about the purpose of the dream.

▶ *Joseph became envied:* The two men then remembered their prison friend Joseph and told Pharaoh of him. Then Pharaoh ordered his release and sent him an executive invitation to his palace. Joseph appeared before Pharaoh and interpreted his dream.

Joseph was set free and Joseph was appointed the second in command in Egypt. God remembered Joseph in prison and miraculously transformed a man from being pitiful to a man to be envied—even amongst men of a foreign country. The same God is still in the business of transformation and your dream could be fulf lled next!

Just as God can cause one to go from being pitied to being envied so, can God turn a barren woman into a mother of children. God can still change you from a pitied follower to a great world leader. After this came a great famine in the nation of Egypt. The very ones who sold Joseph as a slave had to seek food from Joseph's loving hands.

When the people that betrayed you come back to you and plead for forgiveness what will you do? What about the one that you helped advance to the throne of success, only to have him cursed and abandon you? What about a betrayer who left you in a life-and-death situation? How would you react to their request for forgiveness? Because Joseph knew what was ahead of him, he didn't allow the past to decide his future or destiny.

After a man sins against the Almighty God, he calls upon Him, asks for forgiveness and freely receives it. Who is man to hold sin against his fellow man?

> *"Judge not, and ye shall not be judged:*
> *condemn not, and ye shall not be condemned:*
> *forgive, and ye shall be forgiven"*
> *(Luke 6:37).*

Someone said it is easy to forgive, but too hard to forget. When you forgive the sins of another man, you not only help that person, but you do more good for yourself than you can imagine.

*"And when ye stand praying, forgive, if ye
ought against any: that your Father also which
is in heaven may forgive you your trespasses"
(Mark 11:25).*

Unforgiveness hinders our prayers. As you stand to pray, forgive f rst so that your Heavenly Father can forgive you too. Forgiveness pays all debts, delivers us from temptation, takes away our trespasses, and heals our inf rmities. May you receive the mind, grace, and spirit of forgiveness, in Jesus' name.

Joseph told his brethren not to blame themselves for what they had done to him, but they were still troubled at his presence. They couldn't believe their eyes and ears.

Joseph presented himself as someone sent by God to preserve their posterity in the earth, and to save their lives by a great deliverance.

He made them believe that what they had done was divine and not a sin, as they had believed.

It is to the shame of the devil that he used Joseph's brothers against Joseph. In spite of that, all of Joseph's dreams came alive and were fulf lled, above even what Joseph thought they would be.

Having read this book to learn this missing knowledge today, gather yourself together and check line by line what part of your life is not functioning properly. Apply all the weapons you have learned in this book and put them to work. I pray for heaven's backup for your enviable destiny. In Jesus' precious name I ask this, Amen.

CHAPTER NINE

Push On

We are kept by the unveiling power of God through our faith in action. We engage in one endeavor or another on a daily basis in a search for survival. But as one is going higher, others are failing in life, as if every step they take to move forward results in three steps backward.

A car is overtaken by other cars because it cannot keep up with the speed and pace of other cars.

In life, people's positions are being taken over by others because they cannot function properly to keep up with the demands of their duties.

▶ ***Push On:*** Everyone in life wants to be somewhere in life, but very few know how to get somewhere, no matter the dangers and roughness on the way.

There is no prize to pay for failure in life, but there are many prizes to be paid in order to succeed and stand on slippery ground. It is possible for a man to live his whole lifetime in frustration. You don't need to put in any effort to fail in life, but you need more than physical energy to succeed and be envied in life.

To push it is to apply pressure on an object for the purpose of moving it from one position to another. Pushing could also be seen as expending great or vigorous effort on an object in order to change the position of that object. If you forgot all the junk that lies behind and push on, you will not only gain material rewards, but you will see the abundance of life the Lord has in store for you.

Only you have the choice of moving ahead or behind, God made man the head and not the tail, but why is man not ahead?

"Rise ye up, take your journey, and pass over the river Arnon: behold, I have given into thine hand Sihon the Amorite, king of Heshbon, and his land: begin to possess it, and contend with him in battle."

(Deuteronomy 2:24)

In every society there is always a man described as a giant whose physical or spiritual appearance threatens everyone around. That is the reason every man must push forward to his place of possession. We are too relaxed to push forward to acquire what God has given us to possess. It is only spiritual violence that will continue pushing the secure man to his promised land.

There are too many relaxed men in this day and age waiting for the government to make things happen for them for good. That is why you see more organized protects today than ever before. Stealing has become the business of the day because people no longer think they can acquire anything great by themselves.

Whatever trouble is past, is past; stop crying and thinking about it. Embrace the newness of life God has for you. Don't look back to where God is moving you from. Those who look back will turn to a pillar of salt, like the story of Lot's wife in the Bible. Obey God and keep moving forward until you cross over to your promised land.

God will not do for you what you can do for yourself. That is why you cannot die if you choose to live. You can pick up pieces of stone from the street, but it is a nightmare to pick up a fresh f sh on the street.

Again, to push is to advance or move an object forward, despite the diff culties or opposition that hinders it. Pushing involves a vigorous effort applied on a particular thing towards getting the position or location changed. The act of pushing is also the act of moving because he who pushes must move with whatever he's pushing until they both arrive at the destination. If you see someone pushing a truck, you will know that it takes extra pressure to push a stagnant object. Converting potential energy into kinetic energy requires more than sitting down to draw out images, it requires putting your mind, hands, and legs to work.

Good pushers are serious-minded people who don't give up until the job is done perfectly. Rain or shine, they keep pushing forward. They are devoted and addicted to achieving success. Pushers are award winners who make good use of their down time. Pushers are inventors of ideals. They are champions of life who have insight and answers for the issues of life.

"And Joshua said unto the children of Israel,
How long are ye slack to go to possess the
land, which the LORD God of your
fathers hath given you?"

(Joshua 18:3)

No matter how pressed you feel to pass out urine, when you get into the restroom you still need to focus on pushing out. It won't come out of you until you apply the force of pushing it out. No man makes business phone calls in the restroom when it is time to push out. It is a serious moment that needs attention and commitment. You must be committed and show the seriousness by pushing before any change can be made.

▶ *Joseph the Achiever:* Achievement is not a respecter of environment, color, age, or season. The secret of achievement is in how timely and committed you are in getting things done. While some push for a day and rest for weeks, others are committed to pushing twenty-four hours a day, without retiring. The trials, "failures" and successes of Joseph spread over the last twenty chapters of Genesis, not because he was a favorite son of his father, but because he was the most favored and tireless pusher of all.

The one in a family that people say will not amount to anything good may well be the heroic son if he can apply the force of tireless pushing on. The role of a hero doesn't just come upon someone—it is worked for. I don't know what your excuses are. All you need is what Joseph had to hold onto—his dream. Only your dream can get you out of your stagnant state.

God has made all things available for each of us, so why does every man not get it? It is because many men don't see that truth or believe it to be real. Instead they accuse others of keeping them from getting it.

"Which of you by taking thought can add one

cubit unto his stature?"

(Matthew 6:27)

The more you blame others for your failure, the more you remain at one place. Nobody has enough in life, but someone has something very important for life. Joseph contradicted all the plans of the devil to render him useless in life and became the youngest overachiever of his time.

A rejected stone, after pushing, does not only change position, but it becomes the selected stone. A barren woman, after serious pushing, becomes a loving mother. A beggar, after pushing, becomes the giver. Two singles, after pushing forward, became a couple. A frustrated sports team, after pushing, becomes the winning team. A soldier, after pushing, becomes the hero.

Pushing brings about a change of situation, change of name, and a change of destiny.

"I press toward the mark for the prize of the high calling of God in Christ Jesus."
(Philippians 3:14)

It can never be without pushing. Pushing is all you need to be where you want to be. The pregnant woman carries the child in her womb for nine months or so. On the day of delivery, the child doesn't just come because it is due for delivery and the woman needs more than her regular power to push out the child.

There are benefts in pushing. In the labor room, nurses and the GYN Doctor gather around the mother to be, to give words of encouragement. They say to her, "Push! Push! Push! The baby is coming out. Push hard!" Why? Without the push the child won't show up. The success of life is birth by a tireless push.

▶ *The Local Truck Pusher:* In other parts of the world, there are men who push trucks—local truck pushers. They use handmade trucks to transport goods from one location to another and are paid for their services. At the construction site, workers use wheelbarrow truck to transport cement bags, cement blocks and other construction materials to where they are use.

After the goods are loaded into the truck, the truck pusher faces the diff cult task of pushing the fully loaded truck to its destination, where he will receive his reward. The owner of the goods does not care how the truck pusher pushes the truck to the destination. He or she only cares about the timely delivery and safety of the goods.

The truck pusher sweats and people stand to watch him and mock, but he gives no attention to their mockery because his reward awaits him upon the completion of the contract.

Jesus Christ is ever ready to deliver rewards into the hands of whoever pushes to the end. Your breakthrough is at the mercy of your spiritual violence in pushing forward. You cannot acquire it until you show your desire and ability to handle it.

"And from the days of John the Baptist until now the kingdom of heaven suffereth violence, and the violent take it by force."

(Matthew 11:12)

We are living in a world where only tireless pushers survive. The trouble we face today has always been. From then until now, violence continues to reign in every area of life. Spiritual violence has been the only sure way for the manifestation of God's blessings to be acquired by men, and for him to recover all his possessions. The violence takes it by force.

The world is growing increasingly wicked, day by day and night after night. The world has never been a safe place for anyone. The only safe place is the Kingdom of God; that is for everyone who runs to it.

The push of spiritual violence leads to a change in situations, change in feeling, change in profession, change in name, change in environment, and change in dressing. This push remains the only tool man can use to posses all his rightful possessions. Every man needs a violent heart to forcefully recover all his belongings and to cross the wilderness to reach his Canaan.

▶ ***The Wilderness:*** There is a wilderness for every pusher to cross over. You must f rst identify where you are coming from, then where you are going and f nally, who you are at the beginning of every move in your life. Only the addicted pushers push to their end where divine health, prosperity, breakthrough, favor, and everything else of the Kingdom waits.

There was a blind man named Bartimaeus who pushes into his healing. He heard that Jesus was passing by and started shouting again and again, calling out for Jesus, the son of David, for mercy. He acted on his faith. He believed that if he could shout out to Jesus for mercy, he would receive his sight. His yelling likely bothers everyone around him, but Bartimaeus never quits until he arrives at his victory point. He got the attention of the master healer, Jesus Christ. He did what the Bible said and got it.

"Forsake the foolish, and live; and go in the way of understanding."

(Proverbs 9:6)

Wake up and start pushing forward. Stop blaming the leadership of your country, and the people around you. Start blaming yourself for where you are. You cannot move what you cannot push. There are Pharaohs ever- ready to hold you down in every area of life. If you want to push forward—a tireless push is all you must apply.

> *"And, behold, a woman of Canaan came*
> *out of the same coasts, and cried unto him,*
> *saying, Have mercy on me, O Lord, thou son of*
> *David; my daughter is grievously*
> *vexed with a devil."*
> *(Matthew 15:22)*

This woman was turned down by everyone in her life until she pushed her case to the master's attention. You cannot possess what you do not pursue. She came out of her wilderness to a point where she woke up out of her sleep and pushed into her breakthrough.

A manufacturer, after producing a particular product, needs a serious push to get the product to the targeted consumers. There is success in every form of pushing. No push ends without reward. No dream comes to reality without serious pushing.

Pushers are award winners. They are achievers of dreams, and investors in inventions. They are solution bearers, and they do not live to reign among men, but live for others to live. There is no program for fun or vacation in their calendars. They make good use of all their given time to push ahead. Time investment is the number one priority on their calendar.

You may be surprised to know that Jesus Christ, the son of God, was an award winner in pushing ahead. He was the only man who pushed 24/7 to fulfll His mission on planet earth. He knew His days on earth were numbered and knew not to leave any stone unturned. He was always pushing, day and night, to get his disciples conversant with the tasks ahead.

In this world of wonders, pushers are called successful achievers. They don't give up in any event, even when it looks as if nothing is happening for good. In the life of a pusher, no matter what, he pushes to get the job done.

The salesman in the showroom is an example of a violent pusher. He takes it as a point of duty every day to push the product forward for buyers to purchase. Even when the economy doesn't seem promising, buyers complain about the cost or quality of the product. The salesman still presses on to make sure the buyer falls in love with the product, because without persuading the buyers to buy, reward will not reach him.

The Wonders of Pushing: In a standard operating room, you have the surgeon, surgical assistant, scrub technician, circulator, anesthesia, endoscopy technician and the help nurse all teamed up together to achieve one common goal: a successful surgical operation. Everyone carries out his or her assigned duty to ensure the right medication is being used on the patient. Even when the case looks impossible, they put forth every effort to push to the end: until the patient is transferred to the recovery room, happily.

The wonders of pushing require every hand to be on deck to get an amazing end result. The woman with the issue of blood for twelve years wasn't free until she forcefully pushed her way to her place of healing.

"And a woman having an issue of blood
twelve years, which had spent all her living
upon physicians, neither could be
healed of any,

Came behind him, and touched the border of

his garment: and immediately her

issue of blood stanched."

(Luke 8:43-44)

She was rejected by relatives, friends, mother, father, husband, brothers and sisters, due to her terrible health situation that eluded all medical theories. Her health situation was the worst in her city because it was beyond the knowledge of the physician's of the time and there were no scientif c discoveries that could provide solutions to her incurable health situation. But she pushed to Jesus Christ for f nal solution. The disciples tried to prevent everyone from mobbing Jesus, including this woman. But she continued pushing tirelessly forward.

The interesting part of all this was, when the crowd saw her with a violent face pushing forward to touch Jesus, they gave her way to the master. Her problem gave her express access to her place of freedom—when she pushed.

The story of the lepers also painted a clear picture of violent pushing that resulted in them becoming kings over the land—something impossible to even dare think before. The wonders of pushing require getting ahead, no matter what seems to be blocking the way ahead. You don't know what's ahead until you get ahead.

I don't know in which area you have been denied your covenant rights. You may be afflicted, sexually abused, out of work, divorced, lost of home or car, in prison for a crime you did not commit, wrongfully accused, or paid a debt you never deserved to pay. The good news is that you are still alive. No matter what you lost, God is the reason you have not lost everything. There is another day called tomorrow, which is pregnant. You can never tell what's ahead. Your breakthrough is just a phone call or a step away. All those who rejected you before will come and celebrate with you. Maintain an attitude of tirelessly pushing to your desired destination and you will get there in the precious name of Jesus Christ. Amen

CHAPTER TEN

HIS PROMISES

"And it shall come to pass, if thou shalt hearken

diligently unto the voice of the LORD thy God,

to observe and to do all his commandments

which I command thee this day, that the LORD

thy God will set thee on high above

all nations of the earth"

(Deuteronomy 28:1)

Saints of God, as precious as we are and as surrounded as we are by all the promises of God—we still don't have the God-given eyes (spiritual eyes) to see all the things that are available to us. In every act of God in a man's life, there is a part for that man to play in order to move God to action. Don't sit down all day complaining about how slow God is to act in your situations. It is likely you must act to move God!

As you act (if thou), then blessed shall you be in the city, and blessed will you be in the f eld—you will enjoy the promise of a good life and good living. God has made all things available to us, including our personal belongings and material goods. But God's promises are always accompanied by choices we must make in order to be qualif ed for the blessings.

The God we serve is a God of promise and the interesting part is that He never fails to ful- f ll His promises to man. But there is always something a man must do to move God into performing what He has promised. After you have hearkened diligently unto the voice of

God to do all He has set before you to do, then you will become a qualif ed candidate to be set on high above all nations on earth. Remember what God promised Jacob, to give him the secret treasures of darkness and to subdue nations before him. You shall be the head and not the tail. You shall be above and not beneath. Blessed shall be your basket and your store.

"For with God nothing shall be impossible."
(Luke 1:37)

People and nations have tried in different ways to prove God wrong, but the more they try to show Him down, the more they succeed in telling the whole world how powerful and real God is. With God, nothing is impossible the angel told Mary. You don't need a Master's degree to qualify for that job you applied for— all you need is a Word from God.

Once while interviewing for a job, I told a man: "What you need is in my head and not in that paper" after he had gone through my resume without f nding the reference I needed to qualify for a position I had applied for. He looked at me and simply said I was not qualif ed to be hired for the position due to my past experience.

I looked at him eyeball to eyeball and said, "I might not have what you want on paper, but I have more than what you need in my head," and I walked out of his off ce. Two days later, that same man called me back to start the same job for which he had said I was not qualif ed. I had left him with a word that gave him sleep-less night. God made a way.

"And Mary said, Behold the handmaid of the Lord; be it unto me according to thy word. And the angel departed from her."

(Luke 1:38)

Not until Mary heard all, believed, and began confessing in agreement, would the angel depart from her. The revelation was of no benef t and had no effect on Mary until she spoke it into action. The promises of God have no effect until you speak them into action. The angels can only act when we speak the action. But we cannot speak what we do not believe. Mary said, *"Be it unto me according to thy word."*

We see many verses in the Bible where God speaks His Word into action. When we speak the Word, it commits God to perform what He promised. He is real, so what you speak is what you get. How far will you live life? It depends on how far are you willing to speak life.

Have you not heard that life without vision is barren? There cannot be a harvest without seeds having been planted. Only what goes around f nally settles and stays around.

"But as it is written, Eye hath not seen, nor ear

heard, neither have entered

into the heart of man, the things which God

hath prepared for them that love him.

But God hath revealed them unto us by his

Spirit: for the Spirit searcheth all things, yea,

the deep things of God."

(1 Corinthians 2:9-10)

We must stop living for worldly things and start living for godly things. It is unwise to focus so much on material things which give no satisfaction. No matter the quantities we gather, the more we get, the more we want. God is a loving father who will not fail anyone who truly believes in Him. He has spoken His promises from His holy mouth, as the Almighty God—we can stand on them. God's promises are not like political promises from the mouth of a politician who seeks your vote. God's promises never fail.

David declares in the book of Psalms:

"I have been young, and now am old; yet have

I not seen the righteous forsaken,

nor his seed begging bread."

(Psalm 37:25)

From when He was young, until he made these confessions, the Lord had never forsaken him, nor had his seed ever begged bread. May you never beg again-resist every spirit of begging in you now.

God is unchangeable, the same yesterday, today and forever. He is the same size, same weight, and has the same eyes to see, same ears to hear, and the same mouth that gave you promises. God said His wish for man is to live above all things, to prosper and to be in health—even as the soul of man prospers.

God promised Abraham and it came to pass. He promised Noah and it came to pass. He promised the Israelites and it all came to be. God is not a man—He never lies. He is not the son of man that he should deny himself.

"For I know the thoughts that I think toward you, saith the LORD, thoughts of peace, and not of evil, to give you an expected end."

(Jeremiah 29:11)

So often we spend time crying, pleading with God for silver when He has prepared gold for us. We approach the throne with high expectations from God, but the moment we notice any kind of delay, we become so depressed about our situation that we feel God is not real.

God is a loving father who will not withhold any good thing from His children. Man has been too impatient when it comes to waiting for the appointed time of harvest.

God said that to every time and season on planet earth, there is a reason. You cannot change the season of God to a different time. The law of the harvest says that after planting, there is a waiting time for seeds to germinate and bear fruit before the harvesting season.

What season are you in now? Think. Jesus Christ, even with all the prophecies spoken of Him, still had to mature for a long time (over thirty years!) to qualify for his throne. There came an appointed time and season when all prophecies came into manifestation.

Hard times envelope the whole process of redemption, times when God seems not to be real. Ultimately, it came to the day of days when the man of all people faced the most diff cult time in the history of the human race. Immanuel, the Messiah, the King of Kings, the Lord of Lords, Jesus Christ was made to suffer what he never deserved just to fulf ll the promises of God to man.

CHAPTER ELEVEN

Be Thankful

"In everything give thanks: for this is the will

of God in Christ Jesus concerning you."

(1 Thessalonians 5:18)

"IT IS A GOOD THING TO GIVE THANKS

UNTO THE LORD, AND TO SING PRAISES

UNTO THY NAME, O MOST HIGH."

(Psalm 92:1)

▶ **Give thanks:** It is so fascinating to live
a life with an attitude of thanksgiving. On
the journey of life, thanksgiving is one of the

weapons that keep life in full swing. There are countless reasons for every living person to be thankful to the Creator of the universe. There is also a reason for every living thing to say, "Thank you Lord" for the beginning and the ending of every new day of life we live to see.

Thanksgiving strengthens the soul. It is the rope attached to the bucket which goes deep into the well of heaven to fetch the water of joy. Thanksgiving is the heavenly treatment for depression and anger.

Thanksgiving qualif es a man for divine presence. This is why it is the will of God concerning man, in Christ Jesus, to give thanks always.

The attitude of thanksgiving is all that life needs from every living creature. Thanksgiving is a response of the receiver to what has been received. When we receive and respond with appreciation, it adds value to what is received. Thanksgiving is not fruitful until the gift is put into use. Do not store up what you receive only to build abundance. Use it and share it. It is the giver's will to see the gift in use and bearing much fruit.

"And so he that had received five talents came and brought other five talents, saying, Lord, thou deliveredst unto me five talents: behold, I have gained beside them five talents more.

His lord said unto him, Well done, thou good and faithful servant: thou hast been faithful over a few things, I will make thee ruler over many things: enter thou into the joy of thy Lord".

He also that had received two talents came and said, Lord, thou deliveredst unto me two talents: behold, I have gained two other talents beside them.

His lord said unto him, Well done, good and faithful servant; thou hast been faithful over a few things, I will make thee ruler over many things: enter thou into the joy of thy lord".
(Matthew 25:20 - 23)

Do not store your gift in the closet because the giver loves seeing his gift shared and made manifest. If someone gives you a pair of shoes today, he expects to see you walking and bouncing with joy in those shoes tomorrow.

The very life you have is a gift from God. What are you doing with this precious gift? Every morning you wake up to see a brand new day—another gift from God. What will you do with this new day God has given you? Think.

It is a good thing to give thanks unto the Lord because everything that comes from the Lord is good. He deserves good things from us too. In other words, it is a bad thing not to give thanks to the Lord. Giving thanks unto the Lord is good. After receiving such precious gifts from Him, we must turn back to say, "Thank you Lord!"

Thanksgiving changes one's mood from negative to positive. Those who possess the attitude of gratitude are the joyful. The law of multiplication demands that you trade with what you have to get more of what you need. This also applies to the law of wisdom: "Use What You Have to Get What You Need."

Good and faithful servants are those who multiply their gifts by putting them into use rather than storing them up as keepers of gifts.

Paul said that in everything we do and in any situation in which we f nd ourselves, we should give thanks. This is the will of Almighty God and His beloved son, Jesus Christ, concerning you. God has given life, but to have life more abundantly you must give thanks, no matter how little you have now.

When the receiver says "thank you" for what the giver has given, it moves the giver to give more. Some great lives have been cut short, just because a person did not show gratitude for what he or she possessed. Thanksgiving sets your focus on the giver and takes your mind from the things you don't have. It tells you that what you don't have is not for you (at least not now) and gives you total control over what you have.

In life, not everything that glistens is gold. No matter what your situation is, you ought to give thanks because giving thanks commands heaven's attention. A thankful heart is an active, productive, giving and receiving heart.

Whenever things are not working the way they should, know there is a strong force in action nevertheless and that the only way out is to apply the weapons given you by the stronger force. God said to put on the whole armor of God to f ght what you cannot see.

> *"And Jesus lifted up his eyes, and said, Father, I thank thee that thou hast heard me.*
>
> *And I knew that thou hearest me always: but because of the people which stand by I said it, that they may believe that thou hast sent me."*
> *(John 11:41b – 42)*

Jesus' ministry was a ministry of thanksgiving. He was in constant contact with heaven as a result of his attitude of gratitude. In all the miracles He did, thanksgiving was always his f rst message to heaven because he knew it was the only way to get an express answer from the throne of God.

It seems so diff cult to even say, "Thank you Lord" in some terrible situations, but don't see it as an option. That is just the time when you must say thank you to Jesus even more loudly because it delivers victories.

▸ ***Be Thankful for Life:*** The journey of life is not all the way smooth, it is known to contain ups and downs, good and bad, a time of dancing and a time of mourning, a time of singing and a time of weeping, a time of plenty and a time of lack, a time of planting and a time of harvest. But what happens when you harvest what you did not plant?

The law of gravity says whatever you throw up in the air must come back down, but there are things that come down upon you that you did not throw up, causing you to harvest what you never planted.

"...For with the same measure that ye mete

withal it shall be measured to you again."

(Luke 6:38b)

There is never a time in life when you have nothing to be thankful for. Only a giver is eligible to receive from heaven as nothing comes from heaven to the earth, until something is f rst sent to heaven from the earth. It takes the mercy of God to give thanks in the midst of storm.

"Nothing goes for nothing," they say. For anything to come down from heaven, something must f rst go up. He said to me, your source of blessing is your giving, not your receiving. More blessed is the hand that gave than the hand that receives. When I realized this, I changed my giving habits.

The number one reason to be thankful to God is for the life you still have. There are millions of people who stepped into this day with you alive, but they are not living now. Short sightedness is one of the reasons why many cannot see a need to say, "Thank you, Lord."

A man criticized his country for spending ten million dollars for an Olympic competition, because he saw the trophy and said the money spent to get the trophy would have bought over half a million pieces of trophy. He saw the outlook and did not care to know what the return might be. That country's investment was rewarded with a one hundred million dollar return, and "popularity" became that country's second name. The physical appearance might not be what you expect to see, but the return might exceed your expectations.

In a man's life, there is always one area of concern. His life can look so good on the outside, but if the real story is told, something will not be right. Now think about it, while you are dancing, someone somewhere is mourning.

Your time of plenty is another man's time of total lack. While you are blaming God for your worst, someone else is thanking and praising God for his breakthrough. As a family is celebrating the birth of a baby, another family is mourning the death of a child. Some families even experience both at the same time.

In life, as one is jumping with joy, another is toiling in pain. But the will of God for all, no matter the situation, is to give Him thanks. This is where God predetermines the events of life for every man.

"To everything there is a season, and a time to every purpose under the heaven"
(Ecclesiastes 3:1).

For every season of hunger, there comes a season of plenty. I do not know why we cry and complain when things don't go the way we want them to go. Thanksgiving is a seed. Whenever you plant it by giving, there is a reaction from heaven.

Paul and Silas, had they complained when they were in the midst of a heavy storm, might have seen the storm get worse. The moment they started giving thanks and praising God, they were victorious—a reaction that inspires and encourages Christians to this day. We give thanks for things yet to come and things already done. "Thanks-givers" are always in the presence of God, while ungrateful folks are kept beyond the gate from His presence.

"Enter into his gates with thanksgiving, and into
his courts with praise: be thankful unto him,
and bless his name."
(Psalm 100:4)

Giving thanks is what God wants from all of us. Only a fool expects to harvest throughout his lifetime.

The Bible says there is a time to plant and a time to harvest. The biggest troubles we face today are not natural disasters, but man-made tragedies. The problem is no man wants to experience a time of dryness in his life. Such people f nd someone hates them and they think of killing themselves. They do not understand that no man can be loved by everyone all their life. There is a time to hate and a time to love as well.

Life is no respecter of any man, rich or poor, a journey where every participant answers his or her name. In another word it is known as "On Your Own." As one is weeping for being barren, another one is crying for having too many children that leave her no peace.

There is no reason to envy any other because every man has a burden in life. If you heard the untold stories of others, yours would be just too little to bear.

▶ ***Waiting Time:*** There is a time of waiting which is a time of training. The time of waiting is a time of meditation whereby one lives from day to day meditating on what God has promised to come to pass. Faithful is He who has promised to perform. As the Word says,

> *"...though it tarry, wait for it; because it will*
> *surely come, it will not tarry"*
> *(Habakkuk 2:3b).*

Though it may tarry, wait for it—it will surely come. You will not tarry any longer after the waiting time. Waiting time is the time between planting and harvesting. It is a time of expectation. Waiting time might last a little bit longer, but it will not last forever.

There is a reward in waiting. Too many people are waiting with the hope that joy will come one day. My wish is that they will apply the force of faith to really walk into what awaits the "waiters." Since the creation of the earth, God said no man has seen or perceived what He has prepared for them that wait upon Him. "No hurry in life," is what my mother used to tell me anytime I ran out of patience. Life without crisis is mainly designed for waiters.

Those who hurry never made it safely to the end. They drove through red lights and stop signs and kept traffc police busy. There is a blessing in waiting. God has enough in stock for all of those who wait patiently. After a woman conceives, there is a waiting time she must pass through before delivery. She goes through a waiting time as the baby matures within her, thus qualifying her to be a mother.

Only waiters are qualif ed for tips. Remember the saying, "The patient dog eats the fattest bone."

Jesus Christ, even with all the prophecies that describe his personality, had to wait long after His birth for the full manifestation of the prophecies came to reality. God has made His promises, but the manifestation of the promises will not come overnight. The waiting time is a time of nurturing, a time when you must stay awake to water the plant as you prepare for harvest.

"A faithful man shall abound with blessings: but

he that maketh haste to be rich

shall not be innocent."

(Proverbs 28:20)

The blessing of the Lord is for the faithful. God is looking for the faithful and only waiters are seen to be faithful. Those who make haste to harvest what is not mature enough to be harvested are not considered to be faithful.

A man ascended to the mountain of prayer and three days later, he wanted to be richer in anointing than people who had been on the prayer mountain for three months. Those who wait in line for their turn never struggle to receive their blessings. A faithful waiter shall abound in blessings—blessings without measure. Why worry over what you don't have? What you don't have is not yet for you.

Remember, as you cry for not having a pair of shoes, another is crying for not having legs. As you weep for life not treating you well, another is praying to see yet another day. As one is asking for one more day to live, another is preparing to commit suicide. As one is returning from market, others are going to the market. As family members and friends gather at the grave to bury a loved one, there is noise of joy in the labor room for the arrival of a newborn baby.

There was a man who stopped attending Church because his shoes got worn out and he needed a new pair. He believed God for new shoes for over six months. One day, a friend bought him a new pair of shoes and he joined that friend's church where his friend's uncle was having a child dedication service. They got to the church at the time of praise and worship. As they stepped into the church, the man with the new shoes could not believe his eyes. The pastor had no legs, but he was jumping on his two hands, praising God! He found it this man was not just the pastor but the founder of the church. The man returned his new shoes to the giver and vowed never to give any excuse ever again in his life for not serving God.

The period of waiting can be a period of confusion, of wondering which way to go and what else to do. It can seem like a time when life is stagnant. Those who put forth every effort to make life worth living, yet still see nothing working better for them, can suffer depression if they think too much about it. The waiting time is a time of depression as a result of too much thinking. I thank God for those who have been planting and harvesting all their lives without experiencing waiting time. But for most whose stock in life is far different, they must wait, wondering which way to go, what else to do, who to be connected to, and who to talk to. For them, during waiting time, God can seem not fully real.

"For ye have need of patience, that, after ye
have done the will of God, ye might

receive the promise"

(Hebrews 10:36).

Waiting time is a time of patience that after you have done the will of God, (which is planting) you shall be qualif ed to receive the promises of God. Only the patient will survive the waiting time. It takes faith to give thanks in the time of waiting when bitterness rules the day.

The more patient you are and the more self-control you exercise, the slower you will be to anger. The more you claim your "rights" as the reason not to wait, the more vulnerable you will be to anger and frustration, which leads to nothing good.

▶ *Rejoice:*

> *"Rejoice in the Lord always:*
> *and again I say, Rejoice"*
> *(Philippians 4:4).*

> *"My son, give me thine heart, and let thine*
> *eyes observe my ways."*
> *(Proverbs 23:26)*

A heart for God is a heart of joy. No man rejoices in life without possessing a heart for God. A heart for God is a heart of thanksgiving which keeps one focused and strong in the Lord. Let your eyes observe the ways of the Lord and His might. Learn the ways the Lord f ows with the blessings of rejoicing. The heart for God is the heart that calms every storm of life.

Rejoice in the Lord always! No matter what the doctor says about your health—rejoice in the Lord! If a hurricane is coming your way and your house is in line to be destroyed, the Word says to rejoice in the Lord! When it looks so hard and seems so easy to give up—rejoice in the Lord. A woman looked at me one day and said, "Brother Lawrence, it is so hard to let go of a situation you can still see". That is true for every human being but the good news is,

"...weeping may endure for a night, but joy

cometh in the morning"

(Psalm 30:5).

In our night season, it is diff cult to remember that there is a morning coming, and with it—joy. To rejoice is a choice, especially when you can still see or feel the pain of your situation. You can choose to be patient, even when you don't feel like being patient. You can also choose to be kind, even when you don't feel like being kind.

No matter what situation you f nd yourself in, you can choose to rejoice. You are never more like God than when you are walking in joy. Weeping is not all there is to life. A life in the atmosphere of rejoicing is a life of testimonies, dancing and celebration.

"Thou wilt shew me the path of life: in thy presence is fulness of joy; at thy right hand there are pleasures for evermore"

(Psalm 16:11).

It is rejoicing that gives express access to the throne where God is seated. A prayer from a rejoicing heart gets express attention from God. A life empty of rejoicing is a lonely life, marked by feelings of rejection at all times.

A life of rejoicing is a life prepared to receive from above, and a dwelling place of the Holy Spirit. A troubled life cannot have any contact with God. That is why I am convinced that there is no great distance between God and man. The only distance lies in a man's heart. No wonder God asked for our heart and for our eyes to stay focused on Him, observing His ways.

A man feels great delight in his system and a great satisfaction in his soul when he lives a life of rejoicing. It pays off to live a life of gratitude, even if there is an economic downturn or bad governance in the country in which you live. Rejoice always my dear.

CHAPTER TWELVE

How to Take Advantage of Every Moment

L ife is made up of moments, and the more you recognize your moment the more you advance and give meaning to your life.

The success of your life is birth by taking advantage of every moment that comes to you, how fast you recognize it and turning it into an opportunity. "… I will not let thee go, except thou bless me" Genesis 32:26. You can turn every moment into your opportunity of change by taking advantage of every moment possible. Moments are not labeled for any particular person—every moment is available for everyone, especially for the one with positive reasoning.

When I was a teenager I used to say things like: "When I grow up I will be the happiest man on earth," "I will attend the best school," "I will take good care of my mum," "I will be great husband and dad," "I will drive the most expensive car," "life for me will be perfect," "all my relatives and friends will not know poverty," and so on. Then one cool morning my mum sat me down and told me the amazing story of the bird called the woodpecker (the bird that pecks holes in trees).

"The woodpecker's job is never completed. Before she can peck all the holes she can in one tree, she sees a bigger and more attractive tree and moves on to peck holes in it. When it came close to the time for the woodpecker's mother to die, the woodpecker would often tell other birds that the day her mother will die, she would peck holes in the biggest tree in the king's garden, where her mother would be buried. But the day her mother died, the young woodpecker developed pain in her beak and was unable to peck trees.

Procrastination has never yielded fruit. Whatever you want to do tomorrow you must start today. If the woodpecker had started pecking all the days of procrastination, other birds would have seen a little evidence put in place for the burial of her mother. Opportunity doesn't come always and is not a guarantee of overnight delivery".

Many are grounded in life not because they are paralyzed, unable to walk, or blind, but because they set their eyes on another man's struggle to live, they cannot see when good comes to take hold of it. Their plan B is that if they cannot make things happen, someone else will. Their entire life's journey is grounded on the battlef eld of life, waiting for someone to push them into the pool of opportunity.

In the same way many are looking for someone to give them f sh, while the wiser few seek a net to start a f shing company. Be wise. The world is waiting for the wise that use any available opportunity to effect positive change, or to make the world a better place. They refuse to be parasites. What takes a wise man just a day to accomplish, the parasite by the pool of Siloam waited thirty-eight years for someone to get him his healing.

Everyone faces hard times in life but in the midst of hard times, good things f y by, settling only on those who can see beyond the present to the future. Global f nancial depression has always existed to some degree, but why does it never affect everyone? Why is it not affecting every nation? Why is it not affecting every Church? Why is it not affecting every business and family? We have no control over what comes to us, but we have absolute control over our reactions and what goes out of us.

"Whatsoever thy hand findeth to do, do it with thy might; for there is no work, nor device, nor knowledge, nor wisdom, in the grave, whither thou goest"
(Ecclesiastes 9:10).

Life is too sweet to remain stuck in traffc too long. Anyone can be anything or anywhere in life if the right actions are taken at the right time. The story of the woodpecker said we should take advantage of every moment that comes because there may come a time when no more moments come—we run out of time.

God has not set a limit on anyone. Nor does He treat anyone as a special individual. Our focus on men and negative confessions are responsible for where we are in life.

What turns a pity into a celebrated envy is taking advantage of the moment. President Barack Obama said, "This is the time of change, the time to write a new page for America and the World. Yes we can." Change only comes when someone takes advantage of the moment and says, "Enough of the same old ways!" Too many things hold us back and hold us down because someone somewhere failed to act.

Whatever your hand fnds to do you must do with all your power. Do not think of failing or succeeding. No boxer becomes a champion in his living room. Stop setting limits on your success. The business world is too wild to enter with self-limitation.

There is a very powerful story of a woman in the Bible who did the unbelievable by taking advantage of one piece of information she knew. She turned that information into an opportunity that changed her entire life into a world of faith. Her opportunity transformed her from a pitiable and rejected woman into a person others envied, a selected pillar that stands out to be referenced—even by the master, Jesus.

"And a certain woman, which had an issue of
blood twelve years,

And had suffered many things of many
physicians, and had spent
all that she had, and was nothing bettered, but
rather grew worse,

When she had heard of Jesus, came in the
press behind, and touched his garment.

For she said, If I may touch but his clothes, I
shall be whole.

And straightway the fountain of her blood was
dried up;
and she felt in her body that she was healed of
that plague.

And Jesus, immediately knowing in himself that
virtue had gone out of him,
turned him about in the press, and said, Who
touched my clothes?

And his disciples said unto him, Thou
seest the multitude
thronging thee, and sayest thou,
Who touched me?

And he looked round about to see her that
had done this thing.

But the woman fearing and trembling, knowing
what was done in her,
came and fell down before him, and told him all
the truth.

And he said unto her, Daughter, thy faith hath
made thee whole; go in peace, and be
whole of thy plague".
(Mark 5:25-34)

In the midst of every storm lies an opportunity to take advantage of in order to reach your long awaited miracle. Storms can keep you away from the king, but storms can also make a way for you to dine with the king, like Joseph.

There is not a successful man or woman on earth who has not once been crippled by the events of life. Many lived and died in hard times, but very few turned their storm into a moment of breakthrough. In the life story of a successful man or a failure lies his secrets—a secret of how he started, and how he succeeded or how he failed.

The story above presents a clear picture of a positive thinker. What was on her mind? What was she thinking? She would touch his clothes, not his hand. She would not hold him or shout out his name as others did. Her plan was just to touch and believe in her thought of healing.

She was not the reason why Jesus went to that city, but she turns the master's visit into her moment by taking advantage of it. For twelve years this woman suffered many things of many doctors. She was rejected by relatives, abandoned by friends, had no job, and had no husband. She lived in the worst depression and f nancial hardship for twelve years. The

devil kept her bound in pain, shame, loneli-
ness, worry, restlessness, darkness, and debt.
Through all of that, she kept her hope alive.

To get what you have not yet received from
God in life, you must do what you have not done
for God. These words changed my life: "If you
want God to do what He has not done for you,
give God now what you have not given Him
before." By Bishop Robert Kayanja who was a
guest speaker in a church building fund raising
at New Life Anointed Ministries, Woodbridge,
Virginia. USA.

Success is not all about fasting and prayer,
it is about acting on information and turning
every moment into opportunity. When I heard
him say this, I had $1,010 in the bank and
wanted to use it as a down payment on a car. I
was believing God for a car when I heard what
Bishop said above. The Holy Spirit ministered
to me, urging me to give all the money to the

church for a building project—and I was to go to the building site to pray on the land all night. That sounded funny to me, but it was a way out of lack. I did and two months later I bought a higher quality car than I had hoped for, with cash—I needed no loan. When we give it all to God, He takes over.

You see, on that day, I believe others were waiting for Jesus to lay hands on them, but this woman didn't wait for miracle to come to her. She was prepared to do what no one else would do. She didn't go there to look for someone to help her talk to Jesus or to book an appointment for her to see Jesus. Instead, she decided to just touch his clothes and her long awaited miracle would come—and it did.

From wherever you are, start now to make things happen. Enough of waiting for someone to give you f sh—get a net and catch them for yourself and others in need. When you do this, those that see your example will be inspired and thank God for your sake. You were not created to be a beggar.

Look at this account of a man who took a step of faith, but was stopped because he allowed the spirit of impossibility to hold him back.

"And a certain man was there, which had an

inf rmity thirty and eight years.

When Jesus saw him lie, and knew that he had

been now a long

time in that case, he saith unto him, Wilt thou

be made whole?

The impotent man answered him, Sir, I have no

man, when the water is troubled, to

put me into the pool: but while I am coming,

another steppeth down before me.

Jesus saith unto him, Rise, take up thy bed,

and walk.

And immediately the man was made whole,

and took up his bed,

and walked: and on the same day was

the sabbath".

(John 5:5-9).

For thirty-eight years this man waited by the poolside for someone to help push him into the pool when the waters were troubled by the angel. Others were there for business. No one was there for a celebration party. This man mistakenly set his focus on his fellow man and never knew when help was available. Thank God Jesus found him, but that was too long for a miracle. He waited thirty-eight years in a row to get what took others a day to get.

In the same way, many have stepped into and missed out on the school of greatness. They couldn't get any higher because, to them, there was no man there to guide them to success (and they did not entrust themselves to God—the holder of all success). Ask them what they specialize in and they will tell you they specialize in "general merchandise," jacks of all trades—yet they are a master of none. A jack of all trades cannot be known in any particular trade. He has no settlement because he is looking into everything possible.

President Obama said, "Change has finally come to America; change we can believe in." He maintained his message from beginning to end. Even when it looked like he was not going anywhere, he never changed his message. But over time, his competitors incorporated the theme of change into their own messages. But they were too late to reach and defeat Obama after he moved ahead. Everyone wanted change. Even our bodies yearn for change when we do not use them productively. The more his rivals tried to scare people with his message of change, the closer people got to know him better. No one succeeds in everything, but everyone can succeed in one thing. Success is somewhere for someone, but not everywhere for everyone. (The same is true of failure.)

Turning every moment into an opportunity is what takes someone from nowhere to somewhere where their miracle awaits. May God bless and guard your steps.

CHAPTER THIRTEEN

The Battle I Never Saw Coming

L ife is a step by step process. In life there are ups and downs, times and seasons when relationships are built and broken, times of a child and times of an adult and times of planting and harvesting. Life is unpredictable. No one can really say what lies ahead. Everyone is going or has gone through something incredibly diff cult because the battle for life is a battle for change and change has no end.

No one survives the battles of life without a physical or spiritual change. Every survivor ended up somewhere and not everywhere. (Those who targeted everywhere never got to anywhere.) The battles of life are everywhere, but why is everyone not experiencing them to the same degree? Just as God has prepared a place of blessing for each man, so the devil has also planned storms for each man.

Abraham was asked by God to go to his place of blessing. Until he got to that place, no breakthrough could occur in his life. The storms and battles of life are eye opening and draw their victims to the place of change. You cannot experience your divine allocation until you can recognize your proper location.

Battles are real and though they knock on every man's door, they cause great damage in the lives of those who are disconnected from their divine location. There is an allocation for the person who answers the call at the right time and relocates to the right place.

There is no airplane that departs from a particular airport to arrive everywhere. It takes off from a specif c somewhere to arrive somewhere.

People face trials of many different kinds due to what others see or say about them. Many are in prison houses, some even in the grave as a result of careless words they or someone said, or due to a negative decision they made.

I became a victim of what people said about me for a very long time. The negative perceptions of others caused me pains of untold hardship. I went through years of setbacks in life as a result. I spent my time concentrating on what people were saying about my future rather than what God had destined for me.

I have faced trials and tribulations, but in all, the Lord was faithful and never failed me.

I never knew the role of a father in the life of a child until I became a father myself. Similarly, no one can enjoy the benefts of the Kingdom of God until he or she receives them.

I was born to a loving couple, but dad passed just a couple months later as a result of persistent battles with men who positioned themselves to be used by the devil to execute evil acts. Life is funny. No single man can tell how good a husband or father he will be until he experiences what family life is all about.

As I grew older, the sense of daddy's absence became real to me. As a child, I often asked where my dad was and if I could see him. When I asked, someone would always tell me he had gone on a very long vacation trip. One day I came to realize that daddy had gone on to the world beyond. From that moment, I knew that growing up without a biological father was going to be tough.

As I grew older, the closer I was drawn to the unseen life. Not too long after daddy's burial, mom became seriously ill and was hospitalized for quite a long time. All these events and happenings trained me and prepared me to be stronger when facing unforeseen events ahead.

I got to know my relatives better as they babysat me when mom's sickness kept her away. Her full recovery took a very long time. As I grew to be a man, I went through hard times and seasons of testing. Growing up without a father is a hard story to tell and a terrible road to travel, but in all of it, I learnt to be dependent on God.

I am living to get over events I have had and those yet to come, but one I went through in 2003 was the most serious. It is still a serious battle for me to f ush the memory of it out of my mind and let it go. I kept this event secret since then. But as God wants it, I am sharing it in this book to save those who might want to follow friend's directives to their graves.

▶ *The Battle:* The year of 2003 was unique. That year, the showers of blessing were all over me. Everything I touched ended up great, no matter what it was. Yet, in spite of this time of great success, the fear of people watching me as if my life was better than theirs gripped me. Fear and insecurity fell heavily upon me. I became convinced I would suffer an attack or untimely death.

Surviving life in this world of wonders takes a calculated strategy. We must possess the drive that sees no reason why life cannot reach its destiny. In life, no one gets whatever he or she needs without tirelessly working at it. You might get what is irrelevant without asking for it, but getting what you really need is more than dreaming. I struggled with events of different forms that pulled me down some ways and raised me up in others.

In 2002/2003 I supported a candidate that was running for the Southeast senatorial district in Rivers State, Nigeria. Politics is a game one can liken to soccer, where every player strikes to win. The successful politician wins a game of calculated numbers. The numbers indicate how well each candidate has done reaching the voters, listening to their views and telling them what they want to hear—not what they need to hear that is right for them. What capture voter's minds and interest is how best the candidate can comprehend the issues most important to voters and the power in the candidate's tongue to address those most important issues. Voters are not captured by the accumulation of material things.

Two opposing teams cannot win the same game. Championship f nals always end with a single team winning. My candidate was the youngest. He was new to politics and inexperienced as a senator. But he was the smartest and most likeable candidate as well as the one with the plan for change that voters sought. As a freshman to the game, he was seen as the one with fresh ideas. Young voters sought this, as the old "faces" had no fresh ideas.

Many vowed not to live to see my team celebrate a win. But the game of politics is one that is no respecter of age. It is not a game of luck—it is for the f rst to cross the f nish line. Elders from the candidate's area went and told the state governor that my candidate should be the one least seriously considered for the senate off ce. On the other hand, I made a blind declaration that he must be the winner. Wonder of wonders, those who vowed not to see my candidate win were the f rst arrivals at the celebration party for his win.

I saw the real wonders of Nigerian politics displayed in the party's primary election, where all the voting materials were withheld and diverted to a hotel by an opponent for over half of a day until God intervened. Information is powerful. The right piece of information is stronger than any weapon. I was on top of every strategy from the opposing candidates. I attended all their meetings remotely by way of wireless connections. I couldn't tell my candidate any of the information due to conf dentiality and integrity.

All those who promised to help us called in sick on Election Day. All the resources apportioned to them were left unused. After many phone calls to try and regain their help went unheeded, we lost all hope. I was with the candidate in his bedroom. We were both thinking of the negative outcome the day would bring. He said to me, "Lawman, let us start thinking of the kind of business to invest in for the next four years as the atmosphere does not look good with all our sleepless nights." But then an hour later, a surprising phone called came in from Oyigbo's local government—it was the beginning of our victory's manifestation.

Before this time I was a show promoter known for having great ideas on how to effectively promote a product to consumers, no matter how unpopular the product. At the start of the campaign, the further we went, the higher and more diff cult to climb the mountain of success became. I saw the battles ahead and believed the only way to success would be by a collective effort from young voters. So I formed a grassroots movement to work tirelessly to sell the candidate to new voters.

Before long, my candidate had gained popularity in the places that mattered most, thus making me a target for the opposition. My name and position became a threat to those who vowed not to see our victory happen. As the general election approached, their plan of attack against me grew from words to physical threats of violence. People began telling me when and where I should not go and who to avoid.

In a game of numbers, everyone matters. The surest way to success was to carry everyone along. Politics is a game of wonders. The same people who are trying to parley (negotiate) with you could turn into your enemies in an instant, becoming an enemy in your house (which is far more effective than a battalion of enemies from afar).

On a quiet Sunday morning after the primary election, I walked by one of our primary opponents near the state government house, Port Harcourt. As soon as he saw me, he pulled over and stared at me until I walked past him to my car and zoomed off. I was scared to death as I walked and drove. I prayed that God would make my back bulletproof because I was wondering what his plan was. God kept me safe. It is easy to escape an attacked you can see, but it takes the help of God to survive the one that creeps up behind you.

A man saw me days later and asked how I was still alive! He thought it was over for me from all he had heard. In his words: "Your name vibrates as if you were a giant (but not). Your name carries weight wherever mentioned."

Another man came to my house early one morning from another city to tell me a deadly dream he dreamt about me. He advised me to be very careful during the election. My eldest sister called me one day in tears, telling me her fears for my safety had become great. She ended the call saying, "My brother, heaven helps those who help themselves." I tried to forget those scary words, but they kept popping up in my mind.

I woke up one day and ran to meet my spiritual mother in the Lord, to tell her my situation. She only made it worse, telling me, "There is a sign of danger ahead of you, but nothing is too hard for God to do if we ask of Him."

She put herself on a seven day time of prayer and fasting on my behalf. The best part was when she asked me to stay inside in fasting and prayer throughout the week of the elections. To me, that assignment was like opening the door for defeat. I decided not to stay behind closed doors. I was prepared for either good or bad. The devil took advantage of that decision and gave me a fast, shortcut connection that almost ended my life.

▸ *The wonder Forest:* On Friday, April 11, 2003, the day before the senate election, I took a f nal campaign trip to places that mattered most for us to win the race. (I was continuing to utilize underdog tactics.) While driving through the village Kanni, a man with us named Judah diverted us to a spiritual Indian professor that he described as a strong pillar of support for one of our opponents. This was a man he wanted me to see from the beginning of the campaign, but I was never moved to see him. He even gave him my personal contact information, but I turned down all his attempts to meet with me.

When we met with the spiritual professor, Judah introduced me. It was soon clear the spiritual professor wanted to speak to me privately. He collected the gift we presented and took me aside. He recounted the game plan of his candidate to end my life on this planet on Election Day (the following day). He said he had heard much about me and spoke of how important I was in the campaign. He said my name was ringing everywhere as if I was the candidate himself. He asked me to follow him to a basement he used for his psychic business. He saw that I was very uncomfortable and was about to leave, so he quickly asked me to go, but to return back at midnight with someone I trusted. At that time, he promised he would reveal more information to me.

That sounded good to me, so I left and returned back as agreed. When we arrived, he offered to give me something to help me escape any physical attack I might face. I turned this down because I had never used any form of life protection before then, but he insisted that I accept it for just one day and return it back to him at the end of election. I asked to see what it looked like. He took us to a nearby forest only after I agreed to use it for one day. The fear of attack and death were heavy on me.

There in the forest we all took oaths not to reveal my source of power in any battle. We returned back to his basement. He brought out a book, raised it up, invoked my name and the gods of India seven times, and f nally opened the book. A f ashy rope fell from inside the book. He said: "I love you, seeing how young and good-looking you are. I've done this for great politicians. I am not asking you for blood or for you to put marks on your body. All I am asking of is that you carry this rope with you."

He mentioned known politicians he had helped and asked me to pick up the rope for two thousand naira (twenty dollars) which I did. He warned me never to let the rope get away from me on the day of election. He also told me to stay alone, to avoid having sex, and not to ride in a car with any woman while I had the rope. Finally, he told me no one should see or touch it and that I must be sure to return it to him immediately after the election.

This all sounds so stupid now (and I know it makes me look so naïve), but back then it was the only way I knew to survive the unseen battles ahead. I was so desperate to survive the attack after all the rumors, dreams and feelings I had heard.

(Thank God, collective prayers from believers moved God to intervene. In fact, so powerful was God's response that the evil professor surrendered all his dark spiritual forces and joined a Church. He now knows the truth of God which has helped him to live.)

On Saturday, April 12, 2003, I drove the entire time from when the election began until the closing of all. I went looking for battles I was told to watch out for. My f rst encounter was in a community called Wiiyaakara. Everyone in my car was evacuated at gunpoint. I drove many miles in reverse to alert the police and gain reinforcements to rescue my passengers-thereafter we went to Okwale town to rescue a commissioner who had been locked up by community youths. I wanted to see how that mystic rope I carried would defend me in battle before returning it, but I was not involved in any personal attack.

The election ended with a win for us, but the tiny rope in my pocket wouldn't let me celebrate the victory. I walked into a battle I never saw coming. I became abnormal from the moment I received the tiny rope from the evil man. I felt so tired and looked worn out. I was unable to act as I normally did. I was under a covering that was like a heavy weight and I could not share it with anyone.

I refused to return the rope as agreed. I wanted to try it again on the next Election Day, the presidential election on Saturday, April 19, 2003. I wanted to prove its power once again. Thank God I didn't return it that very day, because men were on standby to take me down once I showed up. Because I had delayed, the evil professor sent his men after me on the presidential Election Day.

Around 4:45 p.m. that day, a guy approached me and introduced himself as being sent by his boss to stay with me for the rest of the day. I stupidly let him into my car, after I conf rmed his source. Later in the evening he demanded that I return the mysterious rope. We were stopped in a remote area when a man drove up on a motorbike. They both forced me to join them outside the vehicle.

I was taken to an unknown place and held captive for three days, from Saturday, April 19, 2003 to Tuesday, April 22, 2003. I came back to my normal self after evil professor took back the mysterious rope from me the next day, Wednesday. I then learned that their strategy had been to trick me into a f ght so they could kill me in "self defense," thus eliminating me on Election Day to claim victory. God had turned this around in my favor.

According to an insider, assassins awaited me on the way from the evil man's house the very night of the Election Day when he had invited me over. But the men fell into an argument amongst themselves and missed me when I passed by. He tried all he could that night to delay me, but I told him to do quickly all that he did. At the time, it did seem he seemed to be expecting people, but no one showed up. My God is too strong and ever present.

The one who offered me security turned out to be a killer. Only the Almighty God knows what is hidden in this world of wonders. I thank God for His grace.

▶ ***The Wonders of Life:*** "Show me your friends and I will show you your future." Whenever you fall into a battle you did not see coming, look very closely and you will discover an insider had a hand in it. Many have ended up in graves, hospitals and prisons not for what they did, but for crimes committed by a close friend. No armed robber can break into your home to steal or kill without an insider who knows the security system in your home or who has insights into your routines.

The man Judah, who took me to the evil man's temple, actually went into hiding all through the period of the planned attacks on me. Then he just showed up at my house one day. I had already been overtaken by the spirit of forgiveness toward him.

When a man dies, watch for the one who cries most. The elders say, "Whoever cries more also laughs more."

Many years ago, a man received a phone call from a female friend to meet at a certain place for a date. He quickly dressed up and told his wife and f ve children that he was going out for a political meeting. He would be home in three hours. He kissed his wife and left. Five hours later his wife received a phone called from a mortuary attendant who asked her to come and identify her husband's dead body. He had been hit by the wonders of life. And that was how his journey of life ended in cold blood.

Over the months following the attacked, I got to know the part each of the campaigned colleagues played in the plan to end my life. We were doing almost everything together as friends, but little did I know that my life had been sold out for cash and I was surrounded by wonders. I keep wondering what would have happened had they used a different strategy for ending my life.

I was recovered from the evil professor's house by a brother. It took me months to put my shattered life back together. For three days I had been held captive and denied food, water, and freedom of movement. The news of my attacked became the talk of the town. Wonders started all over as news about my kidnapping and conf nement were spotlighted in the news. But in all of that talk, no one came to ask what really happened.

I saw myself with eyes open, swimming in a heavy battle I never saw coming. I was most surprised by the reaction of some of my closest friends. They came to me in the name of thanking God for my survival, but left sharing false words I had not said and spread gossip. All the time I was silently thinking about my broken life, others were running from pole to pole using my situation to get attention and favor for themselves.

Wonders of life visited me and I suffered the worst rejection I had ever endured from relatives and friends. I was left all alone in life to the extent that I thought even God had rejected me—for I had not taken the advice of the woman who had advised me to stay put, fast and pray.

Life became unbearable and full of wonders. All my friends who formerly ate, drank and celebrated with me now turned their backs to me. I sat quietly for months thinking how in the world I got into all that mess! I kept asking myself what I was thinking that caused me to become so lost, causing me to agree to accept that mystical rope. All in all, I knew and saw things that would've taken me a lifetime to discover otherwise.

Now I know which people mattered the most to me, no matter how near or far they were from me physically: from family, to the altar, and even on the job.

One could be the Director General of the Secret Service and still not be able to f gure out who his enemies are using only his physical eyes. We should sometimes pray to have a storm to reveal our true friends and those who matter most.

The world is full of wickedness. When we are in a comfort zone—that is when we must be the most alert. A man who walked with Jesus Christ also sold His life for cash. When a married man or woman departs, the woman or man closest to the family always seems to end up being the replacement.

Still thinking and trying to overcome the entire event, the devil now used a blood brother to openly show me what life contains. He vowed to teach me an unforgettable lesson I will ever live to remember in life. He petitioned the police that I had plans to murder him, then to end my own life in prison.

A few days before I was arrested, someone in the camp carelessly reported me saying one morning that "Lawman will leave his house one morning, and would not return back". The police investigated but could f nd no fault on my part. The funny part came when a friend who was paid to testify against me saw me at the police station and took off running away! The same police off cer who was given orders by the police commissioner to jail me later became the man God used to tell me the entire plan that had been laid down to frustrate me in life.

When people who do not know my past see me praising God, they look at me as if I am a madman—dancing out of control and doing all that I do. But those who know what I have been through in life and how God has delivered me; blame me for not doing enough for God or being expressive enough toward Him! God has been so good and helpful to me. Even when I don't deserve His attention, He still sets His eye wildly on my life and family.

After the whole incident, I took time out of the public eye to prepare a payback attack on all who had been in on the plot to kill me. I consulted movies and books, and equipped myself with technical items that would enable me to get take out my targets without becoming a f asco.

▸ *A Surprising Revelation:* It is so easy for one man to start a war it will take a group of people to end because taking apart is cheaper and easier than putting together.

On the very day I planned to begin delivering payback, I ran into a friend. As we started talking, this man told me his personal story— something he had never shared before. He just saw me and started telling me his past stories, of how he was arrested and thrown into prison for crime he didn't commit. He said: "No man's condition is worst and no man's condition is perfect. Some folks go about attacking others for a little thing that could be forgotten."

He knew my story, but He did not know what my plan was on that day. He told me how amazed he felt to see his achievements in life after surviving a death sentence. I asked him how he had survived—no man survives a death sentence. He said God freed him because he was innocent of the crime for which he had been arrested. He recalled witnessing the executions of prison roommates as he awaited his turn.

The more he talked, the more he had my attention. At a certain point, these words hit my mind, "if this man can live above his past, why am I trying to pay back the assassins and their helpers from my past?" From that moment, I began experiencing a new fresh breath of life f owing through my mind.

You cannot give to another what you do not have. You must possess something in order to give it to another. He was able to talk me into a change of mind because he had the words I needed. He shared my values and provided the hope I sought.

▶ ***Fire on the Mountain:*** Newly wedded couples call it a honeymoon, but to me it was a "Recovery Moon." I spent months trying to get my life together, thinking what the unforeseen days ahead were going to look like. But one day, as I sat doing my usual thing, drinking beer in a restaurant to subdue stress, I was caught red-handed at the scene by heavenly forces.

It was a cool Wednesday afternoon. I dropped off a female friend and on my way home I saw a newly opened restaurant. I decided to give it a try to see if I found a new home away from home. Little did I know that there was a f re on the mountain, just awaiting my arrival to begin burning. When I walked into that restaurant, the last thing I thought would happen was that I would meet a gospel preacher, hear a gospel song, or discuss Bible issues with anyone.

I sat down at a table and the waiter took my order. As if according to plan, the waiter took forever to serve my order. As I waited for the "elephant speed" food to arrive, I suddenly turned my head to my right and saw a framed picture of a handsome young man, standing by a fantastic coup car with his hands in his pockets. The picture drew my attention.

I moved closer to get a better look. Just beneath the image, I saw words I had never read, nor heard preached before then: *"Behold, I am the LORD, the God of all f esh: is there* anything too hard for me?" (Jeremiah 32:27). I returned to my seat but as I sat down expecting the waiter to serve my order, I felt very strange and uncomfortable. In fact, by the time my order was served, I had no appetite. The beer seemed like poison even to taste. I did manage to do consume it. But as I did, I found myself meditating on the words I had read: *"Behold, I am the LORD, the God of all f esh: is there anything too hard for me?"*

An inner voice demanded an answer of me to that question. I tried to ignore it and just eat my food, but those words keep replaying in my mind, over and over again. I wondered what was going on around me. I became restless. Every part of my body was troubled, and still question demanded an answer.

I managed to control myself and play like a man. I walked out of the restaurant, got into my car, and drove home slowly. The same question was written on billboards! I heard it on my car radio! I began to wonder if I was still myself. I became so tired and afraid of the situation; I thought I would lose my senses.

The further I go, the more I was pressured by those words that bombarded my mind. Then these words too were added:

"Men have failed you. Life now seems to have no meaning to you. Brothers, friends, and relatives have abused and rejected you, but know that I your God own your life. There is nothing too hard for me to do. Come to me and I will renew your life and give you a new hope for a new future. I am all you need to have your needs met if you will obey me and carry my cross. Is there anything too hard for me? You labored for man and gained nothing. In return for your love, you have received hatred and rejection. For your good wishes, you are criticized and punished. Is

there anything too hard for me?" I knew it was God and responded, *"Nothing is too hard for you, my Lord."*

Immediately I was relieved of all my burdens. From that moment, I was set free and began thinking positively. For the f rst time, I released forgiveness to all those who plotted my death and felt like nothing ever happened. New life came into me and I felt a fresh air all over me. From that moment, my entire life changed for good. I saw my mind healed and set free from anger and un-forgiveness. It was set free by my response to the question I was asked.

That Sunday, I found my way to church and reconciled with God. I accepted Jesus Christ as my Lord and personal savior. I was born again to live again. The rejected stone became the selected pillar of the house. That is how I dove in and out of the battle I never saw coming.

CHAPTER FOURTEEN

A Wonderful Easter Sunday

It remains a day to remember. Though it came as a day like every other, one thing made this particular day unique.

(No one can give you what he or she does not have. No one can advise you on any situation he or she has not gone through.)

This is a testimony I wrote in the recovery room after my wife was operated on and taken from the operating room for a C-section at INOVA Fairfax hospital, in Virginia, US. I wrote this as I sat by her bed facing one of the most diff cult storms of our lives, knowing that there is always victory in every storm if Jesus Christ is in the boat. (Having Jesus on your boat does not mean storms will not come, but it gives you an automatic victory over the full power of the storm.)

March 23, 2008 - it is my birthday and also an Easter Sunday. I have experienced situations upon situations in life, but in all, I have never allowed the present or the past to dictate my destiny. I try not to allow feelings to get me stuck in life. But folks sometimes push some dangerous buttons that make me crazy, causing me to recall past experiences I try to forget. How would you feel after spending years helping folks to come to a day when you need help, but no one is there to help you? I pray for folks on every kind of issue, no matter the distance, on the scene, or over the phone—and these result in testimonies. But when it comes to my personal need, I battle all alone. Sometimes

I get immediate answers on different issues. God uses the delay method to test and prepare me to see how obedient and committed I am to Him. "Delay," they say, "is not denial."

▸ **Knowledge:** *"My people are destroyed for lack of knowledge" (Hosea 4:6).* God knows the importance of knowledge, which is why he aired the statement above. Bishop David Oyedepo once testif ed of returning home to be told by his wife that she had a miscarriage. He responded by saying, "Give me my food." That was the end of it. There was no recall on the topic—until the supposedly miscarried baby was delivered.

When my wife was about two months pregnant with our f rst child, she called me one day from her off ce to say she had just miscarried. Immediately I responded, "You are f ne," and ended the phone call. She got home at the end of the day and we greeted one another, but she kept looking at me until she finally spoke.

"Why do you never take anything I tell you seriously?" she asked.

I looked at her and repeated, "You are fine," with every ounce of faith. We had the baby.

When my wife had arrived home that evening, she expected me to tear heaven open with prayer as usual, but my understanding was more than prayer, due to the knowledge I had gathered from Bishop Oyedepo's testimony on the same topic.

There is no weapon as powerful as knowledge. No wonder a soldier is well-trained with sufficient knowledge practice with weapons he carries before he is allowed to use them. Without knowledge, one can become a victim of one's own weapon.

► ***Look unto God:*** There was a man of God who served as my first spiritual father, who I respected greatly. But a day came when I needed some anointed words from him on a pressing situation. I sent him an email, expecting a word concerning the situation. In my email I explained to him how God had answered my prayers for others so fast, but delayed when it comes to prayers I uttered for my personal needs. He refused to reply to my email and even pretended never to have received it. Because he behaved in this way and acted this way at a time when I needed him most, I redirected my concerns to God.

I went back to God to ask why the man had failed to respond to me. God told me what I had never heard Him say before then. He said, "Stop looking unto man for help, and ask for help from above." No man had the answer I needed.

► ***The Journey to Destiny:*** To obtain a higher education degree, one must pass from lower grades to progressively higher grades by completing specif c coursework successfully, thus achieving a degree. No one acquires a degree by skipping classes. The journey of life is a step by step journey, not a leap by leap, jump by jump journey—it's all about one step at a time. God ordered our steps, not our running or jumping.

When we are taking one step at a time, God guarantees He will work with us for a successful and victorious journey to an expected end. Those who journey with God never fail in their walk with God. When you journey with God, He shows you greater places and mightier things you had no clue even existed. Those who journey with God depend on God. They don't look back or question God. When you journey with God, your connection with the throne becomes constant.

▶ ***Heavenly Intervention:*** This is an account of how God used me to recover the lives of my wife and unborn baby. Sunday, March 23, 2008, is a day I will remember as long as I live. When I get to heaven, I would love to meet the angel that was assigned to my family that day—to personally commend him for a mission well done.

Life is unpredictable. No wonder so many people say, "I just saw him or her," after someone dies. They always ask: "What happened? I just spoke with him or her a few hours or days ago!" I would have asked these same questions had heaven not intervened as a result of the direct connection I had with the throne.

My wife, Mrs. NiaBari Blessing Maeba, had just returned home from church on March 23,

2008, when she developed pain and swelling in both of her legs. She called her doctor's office and was advised to go to the hospital. She went upstairs to get dressed up in preparation for the hospital. I was in the living room dressing our first daughter, Miss Faith Baridakara Maeba.

I finished dressing Faith and for over twenty minutes, I waited for NiaBari to come downstairs so we could leave. Suddenly I felt a force pull me from where I was to the bedroom upstairs. I couldn't recall how I passed the staircases, got to the room and saw her lying face down on the floor, dead. She was six months pregnant.

Immediately, I knew something was wrong. I called to her a couple times, but gained no response. Immediately, I tuned to the heavenly frequency (Jeremiah 33:3) and heaven opened. While praying, I saw her face transfigured into something I could not explain. Blood and water gushed out of her mouth.

This happened on a day when I was "charged up" by a book I just finished reading, *Walking in Faith*, by the late Kenneth E. Hagin. Before then, I had always looked for an avenue to challenge the devil and here came an avenue to upload and exercise what was inside me. My mentor, Bishop David O. Oyedepo, in his sermon that morning I watched online said, "Jesus Christ defeated death and rose from the grave so we would live out our full days on earth."

In my prayer, I called for heavenly authority, demanding the four carpenters. They arrived so fast and sprang into action with me. As I applied the name and blood of Jesus Christ, I saw my wife in the spirit realm, trying to say "Jesus" with me, but she could not. I gained more power and continued applying the blood and the name of Jesus Christ. The name above all names transformed the atmosphere of the room. I felt the whole place f ll up with the power of God.

All of a sudden, my wife came back to life saying, "Amen, Amen!" over and over. She opened her eyes and realized she was lying on the floor, recalling only hitting the floor in her fall. Now that she was back to life, I called on my sister-in-law, Mrs. Ayakpoere Maeba, who called 911.

The paramedic team arrived and, seeing the effect on her, tested her and asked her questions to make sure she was conscious of herself. They took her to the hospital for further tests and scanned the baby. Surprisingly, the baby was safe and sound.

What the doctors couldn't determine was how the baby survived the whole time her mother lay dead. The doctors performed many medical tests and still could not point out what kept the child alive in her womb. In so many words they said: "It was a miracle. It must be God." The doctors decided to carry out a C-section to remove the baby. We tried to talk them out of doing it, but they said it would be medically wrong to let the baby remain in the womb.

I sat down by her side in the labor room with this question f ying through my mind, "Why me?"

▸ *Job Worshiped the Lord:* I recalled the story and life of Job in the Holy Bible and how he worshiped God in the midst of a terribly tragic storm. I wished to ask Job one question, "Why did you worship and praise God in the most terrible moment of your life?"

The Lord reminded me of great men who had lost their wives and babies in labor. Then I knew why Job was able to do what he did—turning his tragedy to his advantage.

A man called to wish me a happy Easter while I was with her in the emergency room. I answered joyfully and was praising God as if nothing had happened. He didn't know where I was because I didn't tell him where I was.

In a vision, I saw people buried alive because there was no one to intercede on their behalf, or to rescue them when caught by the wonders of life. My wife and son could have been buried alive had I not known God, just as so many other people perish every day for lack of knowledge.

In that same revelation, the Lord came to me saying, "Do not look at things around you; look above for things you cannot see." In other words, things ahead are greater than things present. Looking ahead is to depend on and surrender all unto God for His awesome acts. Looking unto God is to call on God for His heavenly leadings, which never fail. This event brought out the divine potential in me. As you know by now, the gift of God in a man comes out in his time of storm. The devil struck and God turned it to my advantage.

Our new child's name was Master Favour Lawrence Maeba. He weighed less than a pound when he was taken out of the womb—his condition was the worst in the history of INOVA Fairfax Hospital NICU. But his fast recovery was the most miraculous to be recorded as well. He was discharged before his original due date, without any medical issues. No child of his age can compare to him in any physical capability. At three years old, he is as active as any six year old. That is how God used me to recover the lives of my wife and unborn baby.

Lawrence Maeba

Salvation: I called my auto insurance company one day and asked for a discount since I have been paying for over four years, without calling for help. The lady who took my call said there was no discount for me. I asked if I could cancel the contract and she said, "Nobody needs auto insurance every day, but everyone will need it someday." I think the same is true of those who do not know God. Nobody may think they need God every day, but everyone will need God one day.

The decision to be born again as a Christian is a decision everyone must make. The decision must be followed by action before one qualif es as a citizen of the Kingdom. It is a hard decision to make, but you know that nothing good comes easily. I made the same decision some time ago and I tell you the journey is sweeter every day.

Friends, what would happen if you ate food at a f ne restaurant and, when it came time to pay your check, you found that someone had already paid your check? That's what Jesus did for you and me. There is no reason you need to pay anything. No debt needs to be paid twice. Pray this short and powerful prayer with me, from your heart.

Heavenly father, I confess my sin and come to you in the name of Jesus Christ. Your Word says, "Whosoever shall call on the name of the Lord Jesus shall be saved," and that, "if I confess with my mouth the Lord Jesus, and shalt believe in my heart that God hath raised him from the dead; that I shall be saved too."

You said my salvation would be the result of my accepting Jesus as my Lord and personal savior. Renew my dead mind with the mind of Christ. Now I accept Jesus into my heart because he died for my sin and arose from the dead after three days. Thank you for coming into my heart, for giving me the Holy Spirit as my comforter, and for being Lord over my life. Amen.

You are welcome into the Kingdom of God as a citizen and from today, I release you to go on behalf of Jesus Christ to settle cases for others. You will no longer be a slave. You have all Kingdom authority. No one will stand in your way anymore. Whatever you were not able to do before, now go and start doing them in faith in Jesus' name. Amen.

THE MANDATE

"KEEP THE CANDLELIGHT BURNING"

The Lord says: "The devil is after this generation's youth. He f ghts daily to aff ict them with different kinds of diseases and covers their minds with evil thoughts. It is time for them to wake up out of their sleeping minds and accept my beloved son Jesus Christ as their Lord and personal savior. The same way I spoke to Peter is the same way I have spoken to you."

"Write the things which thou hast seen, and the things which are, and the things which shall be hereafter"
(Revelation 1:19).

"Tell them my time is near. Whosoever shall confess that Jesus is the Son of God, God dwelleth in him, and he in God. Marvel not my Son, if they hate you. Evil pursues sinners, but to the righteous, good shall be repaid. The time is near."

ABOUT THE AUTHOR

Lawrence N. Maeba studied to be an internet specialist at the Stratford Institute, Washington, D.C. He studied computer net-working and security at The Banner College, Arlington, Virginia. He obtained a second degree in Computer Networking and Security from Anthem College, Phoenix, Arizona, as well as a degree in Information Systems Security (ISS) from ITT Technical Institute, Springf eld, Virginia. USA.

Lawrence Maeba is the president and founder of Enlarged Hardwares, Inc., the home of everyday technology.

His knowledge of Christianity was gained through the Word of Faith Bible Institute (WOFBI) Living Faith Church Worldwide, Inc., Nigeria. He is the founder of the Nia-law Foundation, a non-proft organization that depends solely on heaven-sent supplies, aimed at empowering youth. He also founded Covenant Seed of Restorations, which aims to win souls for the Kingdom of God at any cost.

He is married to NiaBari B. Maeba and they are both blessed with their children: Ms. Faith Baridakara Maeba and Master Favour Lawrence Maeba.

Lawrence Maeba has the God-given mandate to teach Scriptural success through television, seminars, and motivational books on healing, deliverance, salvation, and spiritual breakthrough.

OTHER BOOKS BY THE AUTHOR

The Mind is a terrible Vessel to waste

The Wonders of Life (The Battle I Never saw Coming)